574

THE

ST JOHN'S COLL

GW00734185

HISTORY PRIZE

PRESENTED TO

JAMES SNELL

FOR DETERMINED AND
ACCURATE WORK

SUMMER TERM 1975.

MJMP.

THE AUTOMOBILE MAN

THE AUTOMOBILE MAN

The Story of Henry Ford

JOHN ROWLAND

Illustrated by Tony Hart-Fry

LUTTERWORTH PRESS
GUILDFORD AND LONDON

First published 1974

For
MY WIFE MARGUERITE
Remembering the first car that we shared—a Ford!

ISBN 0 7188 1926 8
Copyright © 1974 by John Rowland

Printed in Great Britain by
The Bowering Press Ltd.
Plymouth

CONTENTS

The author and publishers wish to express their gratitude to the Ford Motor Company for its help in supplying illustration references, and to thank in particular Fords of Brentwood, Fords of Dagenham, and the Ford Archives at Dearborn, Michigan.

CHAPTER ONE

THE BOY IN THE SHED

"Henry!"

No answer.

"Henry!"

No answer.

Mrs. Mary Ford was annoyed. Working in the big farm kitchen in Dearborn, not far from Detroit, she was to some extent dependent on her son's help. She was kept busy enough herself, with cooking, baking, washing and all the other chores of most farmers' wives. She was also, as was usual in those days nearly a hundred years ago, accustomed to make jam and bottle fruit, as well as to feed the chickens and pick apples, pears and other fruit in season. Her husband was always busy on the farm, for he grew many sorts of grain, as well as potatoes, turnips, beetroot and other vegetables. Moreover, there were a dozen or so cows to be looked after, for butter provided a valuable addition to the family income. A husky young son was a useful source of extra labour.

"Drat the boy! Where's he gone? In that old shed of his again, I expect, fiddling with some of his stupid old bits of machinery." Mrs. Ford muttered these words to herself, knowing that there was no one near to hear her. The farm-hands were all out at work on the farm, which extended to nearly two hundred acres. Her husband was down feeding the pigs which he had recently started raising. She wanted Henry—and she wanted him badly.

She went to the door, opened it wide, and looked across

7

the yard to the little wooden shed where she was pretty sure that her son was busy on his own affairs.

"*Henry!*" she shouted at the top of her voice.

"Yes?" An answer came at last from the interior of the shed. "What do you want?"

"Don't you know that it's time to fetch the cows in?" she shouted. "It will be getting dark soon, and then you won't know where to find them."

"All right," Henry said in a slightly disgruntled voice. "I'll be with you in a minute. Just let me finish the job that I'm doing here."

"Don't be long, then." Mrs. Ford came back into the kitchen, and stirred up a nourishing stew which she was preparing for supper. The vigorous way in which she plied her wooden spoon showed that she was still annoyed with her son, and so did the way in which she grumbled to herself. "Him and his jobs!" she said. "How does he think we can make the farm pay if he is always busy with things that may be fun, but don't bring in any dollars?" And she stirred on.

The kitchen, though it was big enough to serve as a living-room also, was cosy enough, with its broad open fireplace, above which hung some cooking pots. This was soon to be replaced by a big iron stove, then thought to be the last word in modernity.

In spite of such attempts to introduce modern innovations, Henry was not always impressed by the way things were done on the farm or in the house. Years afterwards he was to write of those days: "My earliest recollection is that there was too much work in the place." And in saying that he was thinking of others as well as himself. From the moment when he had gone to school in 1871, when he was a little over seven years old, he had come to think that a farm should, somehow, be better organized.

In his little shed across the farmyard, Henry did all

sorts of things—mainly, even when he was quite young, mechanical things. There were matters at school which he thought could be better managed too. The schoolroom, for example, was heated by a big stove which burned wood. It used a great deal of wood, all of which had to be chopped by hand, and the punishment for an unruly boy was to order him to be at school at seven o'clock in the morning, to get in wood and light the stove. Henry did not often have to do this unwelcome task. He was a hard worker at school—and, unlike many young boys, he thought that his teachers were working equally hard in forcing the rudiments of knowledge into the heads of their pupils—but he also enjoyed many activities outside school. Many of the things outside school which gave him food for thought, however, were practical problems.

Near the school there ran a fast-moving creek. In the rainy part of the year this creek became a raging torrent. And often Henry would stand on the bank of the little stream and watch the water rushing by. Here, he told himself, was a source of energy. He remembered the miller's place, not far away, where a water-wheel was pushed around by the flow of the stream, and used to drive the mechanism that ground the corn into flour. Why not dam the little creek by the school, he asked himself one day, and fix up a water-wheel, so that the rush of water from the stream would turn it?

He put this idea up to some of his school friends, and they readily agreed. So a series of rocks and stones was soon piled across the bed of the stream. Turf was laid on top of the stones, and a fairly serviceable dam began to take shape. Meanwhile Henry, working in his shed at the farm, had nailed together some pieces of wood, making a water-wheel with paddles set in what were, he thought, the best positions to catch the flow of the water. He struggled to carry his wheel down to the stream. He

9

put it outside the school, and that evening, when the boys had finished their lessons, they put the finishing touches to the dam, leaving a gap for the wheel. Henry carefully erected the wheel in the chosen position, fixing it in place with wire.

The boys watched breathlessly. The water began to flow into the mill-race, and soon the wheel was spinning merrily around. A little cheer came from them as they saw that Henry Ford's first piece of engineering worked.

Henry and his friends dammed the creek by the school and fixed his home-made water-wheel into place

Then one of them said. "Hi, Henry! Look back there!"

Henry looked. Back from their dam the water was piling up. And as it piled up it was flooding some acres of farm-land, planted with early potatoes.

He was scared at the sight. And he was even more scared when he heard a sudden roar of rage, and saw the farmer who owned the crop of potatoes tearing down the hill, with a big, thick stick in his hand.

Mr. Bush, the schoolmaster, came out of the school building in surprise. "What's happening?" he asked.

"These young rascals have flooded my potatoes!" The farmer flourished his stick in a threatening manner.

"What did you do, boys?" the teacher asked.

"Please, sir," answered Henry, "we wanted to build a water-wheel. That's it over there." And he pointed to the place where the wheel still spun.

"Whose idea was this?" Mr. Bush asked.

"Mine," said Henry. He was never a boy who would try to lie his way out of a scrape of this kind.

"Off with your shoes and stockings, boys," the teacher said. "That dam has to be pulled down—and pulled down as quickly as you know how. We can't have those potatoes washed out of the ground."

The next day, when the ground was beginning to dry out, the boys were given a special lesson on the way everyone should respect other people's rights and other people's property. For Henry Ford that lesson was not really needed. But this little adventure with the water-wheel rubbed into his mind the thought that it was never good to embark on any course of action until every possible aspect of the matter had been studied.

There were other problems that he thought about in his little shed when his father and mother would have preferred him to spend his time on some task on the farm. Sometimes they would find him sitting deep in thought, to all appearances doing nothing at all.

He was in some ways a good farmer's son. By the time he was twelve years old, for example, he was able to help with the ploughing. But his thoughts were not really on

11

the work of the farm, though he knew that it was his duty to take his full share.

The task he found most frustrating of all was the pulling up of countless buckets of water out of a deep well. In the end he persuaded his father to install a pump. Mr. Ford agreed, when Henry proposed the idea, that it was a good scheme. But even so the pump had to be worked by hand for long periods each day, and each bucketful of water had then to be carried by hand to the place where it was needed, whether to satisfy the thirst of the animals or the Fords themselves, or to be used for cooking or washing purposes.

Henry used to go into Detroit, nine miles away, on occasion. And if he went into a cheap restaurant to get a meal, he would wash his hands under a tap. Why, he asked himself, could they not pipe the water round the farm? He learned a little ancient history at school, and was interested to hear about the Roman aqueducts—those channels built to carry water across the countryside. Could something like that be worked out, so that the water from Detroit could be brought to Dearborn?

He was not lazy; but he thought many things which were taken for granted in nineteenth-century America were hopelessly wasteful of labour. His father owned a mowing machine which was drawn by horses. The farmhand simply sat on the machine, steering, while the horses did the hard physical work. Henry thought that this was the proper modern method. The ancient method, on the other hand, was the way in which hoeing was still done—back-breaking labour by hand. Sometimes as he sat in his shed, he wondered if it might not be possible to devise a hoeing machine as efficient as the mowing machine. Why not?

But in his spare moments Henry was a very normal boy. He liked fishing and swimming—and there were plentiful opportunities for these in the neighbourhood. He became an expert skater in the winter months. He also had a dog, of which he was very fond. When the dog died he never had another one, for he had felt its loss so much.

When Henry was twelve years old, there was a second, and far more tragic, loss. Mrs. Ford died, and a married cousin of the family, a Mrs. Flaherty, came to look after the family, until Margaret Ford, Henry's sister, was able to take on the work. After his mother's death, Henry seemed to some extent to shut himself away, devoting himself to his experiments with mechanical things. He took to haunting the blacksmith's shop in the village. Sometimes the blacksmith would ask him to pump the bellows which pushed air into the fire and made it burn more fiercely. Henry was only one of a number of school-boys queuing up to do this task, for it gave them a great thrill. There came a wonderful day when the blacksmith said to him: "Henry, my boy."

"Yes?" Henry said inquiringly.

"Could you hold a horseshoe in the tongs while I hammer it into shape?"

"I . . . I think so." Henry was almost diffident at the suggestion for, though he had often seen the smith hammering a horseshoe into shape until it was the exact size required, he was not certain that he would be able to hold it firmly enough. And if he failed, it would mean that the shoe would not fit. It would be wasted, and so would all the work that the blacksmith had put into it.

"Have a try!" said the blacksmith.

Rather nervously, Henry picked up the tongs, gripped the red-hot shoe, and then watched as the blacksmith wielded his massive hammer.

"In the water now, boy," the blacksmith advised him.

Henry plunged the shoe, which was still red-hot though not glowing so brightly, into the water. Then the black-smith seized the tongs rapidly from him, tried the shoe for size against the hoof of the horse that had been patiently waiting, and plunged it into the water again to cool it down thoroughly.

That was a great day in Henry's life. He had helped to make a horseshoe! And soon he was helping to make all sorts of other things, for the local farmers came in with broken tools and plough-shares. Sometimes—perhaps the most exciting task of all—he would help to make an iron tyre; this was slipped over a cart-wheel while still hot, and then plunged into a great vat of water, so that it contracted and gripped the wooden wheel once and for all.

The Dearborn blacksmith was a kindly soul. He saw that Henry was a boy of real mechanical skill, and he was only too glad to give such a boy a few hints about all sorts of matters connected with working in metal. Meanwhile, at home on the farm, Henry was picking up a good deal of knowledge of carpentry. If the handle of a tool broke, for instance, he or his father would make a new one. Much of the furniture in the farmhouse, likewise, was home-made.

So, after a time, Henry's shed came to look like a fairly simple engineering workshop. He had managed to persuade the blacksmith to let him make some metal tools. He built a forge, a smaller version of that in the blacksmith's shop. The bellows were home-made, and, like Henry's water-wheel, they worked. Then he managed to pick up a little anvil cheaply.

By the time all this had been achieved, his father began to see that perhaps the hours which Henry spent in the shed were not wasted. He could now make a good job of repairing any tool on the farm that got broken. Soon neighbouring farmers and their workers acquired the habit of bringing broken implements for Henry to tackle. They did not seem to think it odd to be taking these things to a young boy—for he was so thorough, and he did the jobs so well, that no professional carpenter or blacksmith would have done better. He did not do these things for money, but for the fun of it. If anyone said: "How much do you want for the job, Henry?" he would reply "Oh, don't worry yourself about dollars. I'm only too glad to be of use."

Some conscientious people, however, thinking of what such work would have cost had they taken the broken tools into Detroit, insisted on giving him something for his pains. Then, on the first day when he could manage to snatch a few hours off, Henry would go into Detroit and spend his earnings on buying new tools or on laying up stocks of timber or metal which he knew would be needed sooner or later. On one of those visits to Detroit—this time with his father—he saw something that excited him more than anything else that he had ever seen.

He had been accustomed to an occasional sight of a steam engine being taken to a saw-mill or to some similar place where it was needed. But what he saw on this particular day was a steam-engine which was driving itself along the road. This was a pretty makeshift device. An ordinary portable steam-engine was mounted on a four-wheeled cart. A series of belts and chains connected the engine to the back wheels of the cart so that, as the engine worked, it pulled itself along. It was not a very attractive machine, and it would make a twentieth-century boy roar with laughter. But it was the first vehicle Henry Ford had ever seen which did not need a team of horses to pull it, and it remained in his mind all his life. When he was quite an old man, he said that he could still remember every detail of its construction.

As Henry Ford and his father drove up in their farm wagon, the driver of the steam-engine pulled into the side of the road and stopped. Such mechanical vehicles were very rare, and they had been known to scare nervous horses.

"Stop, Father!" Henry exclaimed.

15

His father, knowing Henry's great interest in machines, guessed what was going to happen; but he pulled up and saw Henry gazing intently at the steam-engine. Then the boy hopped down, and made his way across the road to the driver. He spoke to him eagerly, and the driver, who was very proud of his machine, was pleased to show it off to the young enthusiast. The engine, which had been built at Battle Creek, Michigan, some distance away, could even draw a little cart, loaded with coal which could be used to keep the boiler going. The driver showed Henry how the chains and belts could be disconnected, so that the same engine could be used to work machinery on farms or in mills.

The business that William and Henry Ford had to do in Detroit that day was not very complicated, and that was just as well, for Henry's mind was in no way on the affairs of the farm. His father was a little amused to see that the boy was almost in a dream, as if he were miles, or even years, away. He might, indeed, have been looking into the future, when his name was to be on the front of many millions of mechanical vehicles of many different sorts—though none of them were nearly as primitive as the steam-enigne which Henry saw that day on the way to Detroit.

The next day he sat in his shed, and tried to make a small model of that steam-engine. If a big one would run along the roads, why should not a small one run around the farmyard?

As he went to bed, his model not yet finished, he still found his thoughts returning again and again to this marvel —a machine that would run along the roads without horses to pull it. Long afterwards he was to write that from that moment it was his ambition to build a machine that would travel along the roads as well as that steam-engine had done.

Not many boys of thirteen can see their life's work laid

out for them as young Henry Ford did on that day in 1876. But there can be little doubt that what was afterwards to be called the Ford Empire started on that day on the outskirts of Detroit.

CHAPTER TWO

SELF-TRAINING

It was not long after that little adventure outside Detroit that Henry began to teach himself about something very different. A school friend of his called in one day to consult him. The friend was very worried. He had a watch which had stopped, and he had not been able to start it again. He had done all the usual things, including shaking it violently, but to no avail.

"Let's have a look at it," Henry said—though up to this time he had no experience of mending watches. The jobs that he had done had been concerned with much bigger things—pieces of the very primitive farm machinery which was all that was available to farmers in those days. He was, however, not daunted by the thought of undertaking to repair something so much smaller.

He got out his pen-knife and prised off the back of the watch. Then he examined the watch very carefully, to see if he could decide in his own mind just how it worked.

"Can't see anything wrong," he announced at length. "Looks all right to me."

"Then why won't it go?" asked his friend. "Stopped yesterday, it did, and it hasn't gone since." The boy was almost in tears.

"I'll have to take it out of the case," Henry announced. "Maybe it's only dirty; but I can't clean it without taking it out."

"Take it out—I don't mind," the friend said.

Again Henry Ford looked at the watch with great care.

He saw that the movement was held in the case by a very tiny screw.

"Haven't got a screwdriver small enough to touch that screw," he said after a while.

"Then what can you do?" asked his friend.

"Have to make a screwdriver," answered Henry.

"How?"

"Watch me," said Henry with a confident grin.

He took a nail from a box in the corner of the shed, and then selected a tough file. The head of the nail was too thick to engage the tiny screw, but Henry saw that if he could file it down until it was much thinner, it would be just right to do the job.

He fixed the nail very firmly in a small vice which had been one of his most recent purchases. Then he set to work with the file. He had to work with great care, for he knew that he must produce a very thin edge—but if he made it *too* thin, it would break off, and he would then have to start all over again. His friend was almost dancing with impatience. He had great confidence in Henry Ford; and he was sure that his watch would soon be in working order once more. Henry would not be hurried. He knew that this would be an awkward task. The nail-head got thinner and thinner, and Henry tested it thoughtfully with his finger.

Then: "I guess that's about right," he said, and disengaged it from the grip of the vice.

Turning back to his home-made bench, he picked up the watch, and very carefully applied his nail to the head of the tiny screw. Gingerly, he turned it—and then heaved a sigh of relief. In a matter of moments the screw was out, and Henry was able to lift the movement out of its case.

"What now?" asked his friend.

"Wait," Henry said in a quietly confident tone. He picked up a small brush, and dusted the movement of the watch. Some small grains of dust came away. Then he took another brush, dipped it into a bottle of oil, and touched

19

various cogs and bearings. The wheels began to revolve, and the watch began to tick.

"It's going!" exclaimed his school friend.

"Yes; it's going," said Henry. "Now all we've got to do is to get it back into the case."

Carefully he slipped the movement of the watch into the case again. He picked up the little screw and placed it in position. He now applied his tiny screwdriver again and screwed the works of the watch into place. The back of the case took only a moment to clip on. He adjusted the hands to show the right time and then gave the watch back to the boy.

"Gee, thanks, Henry!" his friend said gratefully. "I don't know anybody else who could have done that."

"Oh, it only needed a bit of cleaning and oiling," Henry said. Secretly he was very relieved that the task had been so easy. If the watch had not started so easily, he was by no means sure what he would have done to get it going. He understood bigger and more massive pieces of machinery; but he had little idea of how a watch worked.

He told his father about this, and William Ford was very proud. He had by now come to see that Henry had a special kind of gift in such matters, and he knew that the day might come when Henry's knowledge and understanding of mechanical things would be very useful.

A few days later, when William Ford had to go into Detroit—this time not taking Henry with him—he came home with a small parcel which he handed to his son.

"Thought you might like this, Henry," he said. "I saw it in a store in Detroit, and bought it today."

Henry tore off the wrappings of the little parcel, and found in it—a watch!

"For me?" he gasped.

His father nodded. "For you, Henry," he said.

"Oh, thanks, Pop," Henry said. "Now I shall be able to find out more about how a watch works."

It was typical of Henry that his first thought was that now he could discover how a watch worked, rather than that he now had something which would enable him to keep an eye on the time.

It was too dark for him to do anything but put his new watch on the table and admire it; but the next day he set to work on it in real earnest. After "repairing" his friend's watch, he had bought two or three small screwdrivers so that he now would be able to work with the smallest of screws.

He took off the back of the case, and looked at the watch, which was working properly. He could see how the main-spring kept the mechanism moving. He looked at the complex series of cogs and spindles which made up the movement. Then he picked up one of his small screwdrivers. Slowly and carefully he removed the works of the watch from the case. Then he unscrewed the separate parts. Finally he had the watch in pieces, carefully laid out on the top of his bench.

Now, he knew, there came the most difficult part of the operation. He put the watch together again, trying to replace every part precisely as it had been when he began. He was horrified to discover that it worked no longer! Had he made some mistake? He looked at the watch carefully. Was that screw put in wrongly? He rather thought it was. So, breathlessly, he took the watch to pieces again. Now he laid each piece down carefully, making a mental note of just where it came from.

The pieces were soon laid out before him. Now he assembled the watch again, paying special attention to the tiny screw which he had thought had been wrongly inserted last time. To his joy the watch started ticking. He had found the secret. Before it grew dark, he had taken the watch apart again, and again had re-assembled it. This time he found it much easier than he had before. And this time it worked just as well as ever.

For the next few days Henry was in his shed whenever he could snatch an odd half-hour from the various duties he was still doing on the farm. He would take his watch to pieces and put it together again, until he knew every tiny part, and until he could almost have done the job blindfold.

One day a neighbour called on William Ford.

"They tell me your son Henry knows all that there is to be known about watches, William," he said.

"I wouldn't say that," William Ford answered cautiously. "But he does know a lot about them. He's always taking his own watch to pieces, and putting it together again."

"And he fixed a watch that had stopped—it belonged to my neighbour's boy," the farmer said.

"Yes; but it only needed cleaning and oiling."

"Still, he knew what to do with it," the visitor pointed out.

"Is your watch wrong?"

"Yes. Won't work for more than a minute or two before it stops again," the farmer explained. "Do you think he would see if he can put it right?"

"I'll ask him," said William Ford. "He's out ploughing now; but I'll ask him when he comes in for his dinner."

Henry was delighted when his father told him.

"I hope I'm able to do it, Pop," he said.

"I expect you will. I didn't like to tell him how good you were with watches—your own and other people's," said William Ford. "But I guess you'll be able to get it working again."

Henry looked at the watch. It was quite a different make from his own; but he thought that all watches probably worked by much the same principles. And when he took it into his little workshop-shed, he found that he could put it right without any real difficulty. There was nothing seriously wrong with it—just a small screw that had worked

22

loose. He cleaned and oiled the works, and tightened up the loose screw, and then the watch was working as well as it had ever done.

Next time William Ford's farmer friend called, Henry handed him his watch with a smile. "I think that you'll find it all right now," he said.

The farmer put the watch to his ear, and heard the steady tick. "Thanks a lot, young man," he said. "What do I owe you?"

"Nothing," said Henry. "I enjoyed doing it."

"You must take something for the job," the farmer answered. "If I'd taken it into Detroit they'd have charged me something for it. Here." And he plunged his hand into his pocket, fishing among the coins there—and then gave Henry a silver dollar.

"It's not worth that," Henry started to protest, but the farmer interrupted him.

"They'd have charged me more than that in Detroit," he said. "You keep it, son, and buy something that you wanted."

"Thanks very much," Henry said. "There's a new screw-driver I wanted. I'll buy that with your dollar."

This was really the beginning of a new line of business for young Henry. Hitherto he had been concerned with mending broken ploughshares and replacing broken tool handles. But now he found that his reputation as a watch-repairer was spreading far and wide. "Take it to Henry Ford," people would tell anyone who had a faulty watch.

It was very rarely that Henry was defeated. Even when some part of the watch had broken through wear or ill-treatment, he was often able to make a new part himself, out of the stocks of metal which he was slowly collecting together.

Not only watches, however, interested him. He always harked back to the steam-engine which he had seen scuffing its way along the road. And his fascination with steam-engines grew deeper and deeper.

There were no self-propelled steam-engines around Dearborn. A number of the more prosperous farmers, however, owned stationary engines which they used to power pumps for water or saws to cut up tree-trunks. Henry soon found out which farms these engines were on, and, when he could get away from his father's farm, he would go and watch one. These engines often broke down, and then Henry would be asked to see what was wrong and to suggest ways of repairing it.

The blacksmith, who had taught Henry so much a year or two earlier, was not in the least annoyed that some of the farmers went to Henry Ford for advice or help.

"Hope you don't mind," Henry said to him once, "but Farmer Jones has asked me if I can put his steam-engine to rights."

"Think you can do it?"

"Yes," said Henry confidently. By now he knew his own skill in such matters.

"Well, if you can do it, you get on with it," said the blacksmith. "I've got as much to do as I can tackle, in the way of tyres for wheels and shoes for horses. Most of the jobs on steam-engines are pretty fiddling, and they don't pay me very well. I can make more money out of horse-shoes than out of steam-engines."

For the most part, Henry found this work on steam-engines fairly easy. The machines were simply built, and, even if some part was hopelessly broken, Henry found he could make a new part without any real difficulty. Only now and then was there real trouble. And then it was not often Henry's mechanical skill that was at fault.

There was, for example, one occasion when he pushed his arm deep into a cylinder. Something shifted, and he found himself trapped. His arm was gripped tightly. With his free hand, Henry tried to find out what had gone wrong, and just how to release himself. The engine had been stored in a barn at some distance from the farmhouse, and, though Henry shouted as loudly as he could, there was no one near enough to hear him.

He fiddled with various parts of the engine—for a long time without any success. His arm was still fixed fast. For over an hour he wriggled about, trying to release his trapped arm. At intervals he yelled loudly, but still with no result. Then, finally, he spotted a little lever. It was not easy to reach it with one arm firmly fastened inside the engine. But at last he managed to push the lever, by dint of some incredible contortions. As soon as he touched it, however, he realized that he had found the secret. The pressure was lifted, and he was able to free his arm. It was bruised and stiff. After that, Henry became very cautious about putting his hand inside any machine on which he might be working.

He was still attending school. But many of his lessons got scant attention; he was always anxious to be off repairing watches or working with steam-engines or pieces of farm equipment. His shed looked something like an engineering workshop by now, and the cash gifts that he got from people he had helped enabled him to buy more and more tools.

When he replaced a broken ploughshare or put a new piston-rod in an engine, he always made a point of keeping the old pieces. He still haunted the blacksmith's shop—he no longer plied the bellows, for younger and smaller boys could be trusted to do that, but the blacksmith had become his friend, and Henry was often able to beg pieces of waste metal. He hoarded such things, for now he had a resurgence of that ambition of a year or two ago—to make a model steam-engine that would run. It was intended to be just like the big engines he had seen.

He had many bits and pieces of metal which he could use to make some of the parts. The great problem was the boiler. In the end he heated some odd sheets of iron and bent them around until they were roughly circular in shape. Then he fastened them together, heated them in his furnace and carried out a kind of primitive welding job, fastening a top and a bottom on by similar means. The boiler was not, he knew, altogether satisfactory, and it was not completely water-tight, which meant that there was some leakage and a considerable loss in steam-pressure. But it was the best he could do with the materials he possessed. The other parts presented much less difficulty. The cylinder was so much smaller than the boiler that it was easier to make it properly circular; but the piston had to work inside the cylinder, and he found it difficult to make this a good tight fit. In the end he had all the component parts made, and all that remained was to fasten them together and stoke up.

Henry was very excited as he looked at the little engine that he had made. It was not very unlike the bigger one he had seen on the road outside Detroit. Though it was, of course, quite small, and no one would be able to ride in it, he hoped to make it move across the yard behind the farm.

He had chopped some logs into small pieces. With these he filled the little fuel-box which he had fitted underneath the boiler. He thought it should not take too long to get up enough steam to send his little model chugging across the yard, so he put one or two sheets of old newspaper underneath the wood and lit them. Then he stood beside his model, waiting for the water to boil.

It seemed to be a very long wait. He could see some steam coming out of one or two leaky spots, but did not feel that this was very serious. The boiler was certainly not leaking badly enough to put the fire out. The wood was crackling merrily as it caught well alight.

Henry put his ear as close to the hot boiler as he dared. He could hear the familiar sound of "singing", like that the kettle in the kitchen made when the water drew near to boiling point. Then there was a bubbling noise—the water was coming to the boil! Was this the moment at which he would see the result of all his labour of weeks past?

He had fitted a little tap which released the steam from the boiler into the cylinder. The tight-fitting piston had been mounted in the cylinder, its upper end being connected by a series of levers to the wheels, so that when the steam pushed the piston, the wheels would be forced to turn and the engine would move.

Holding his breath, he turned the little tap, releasing the steam into the cylinder. Breathlessly he watched the top of the piston-rod which stuck out of the cylinder. Would it work? He hardly dared to anticipate what might happen. And then he saw that it was indeed working. Very slowly the piston was pushed up out of the cylinder. Then the steam was released by a little valve he had made with loving care, and the piston sank again. Slowly the levers connecting the piston to the wheels moved up and down. Slowly the wheels went round. The little model engine, moving jerkily, made a rather unsteady progress across the yard. Henry, its maker, was almost jumping for joy alongside it. It did not move very fast—but it *did* move, and that was enough for him. Just in time to stop it from hitting the wall of the house, he turned off the tap that admitted the steam to the cylinder.

Henry was highly delighted at what had happened. He had now shown himself capable of doing something that few boys of his age could possibly have accomplished. He had built a steam-engine which would propel itself—and he had seen it make its first successful journey. In the years ahead Henry was to see many vehicles of his manufacture prove themselves on the roads of the world. It is doubtful if any of those gave him the satisfaction which he got from that first steam-engine.

Hurrying into the farmhouse, he called his father.

27

William Ford was busy at his books, working on the farm accounts.

"What is it, son?" he asked.

"Come and see! My engine works!"

William laid down his pen. He did not really understand this son of his, but he knew that there would be no peace until he had seen the steam-engine in action. So he made his way out into the yard.

Henry pointed to the engine proudly. "There it is," he said.

"And what will it do?" asked his father.

"Look!"

Again Henry turned the tap that released the steam. Again the piston moved up and down. Again the wheels revolved. Again the engine moved forward. It was slow and somewhat unsteady, but it moved.

Henry's father looked at it, not unduly impressed.

"What do you think of it?" Henry asked.

"Not bad."

"Not bad!" Henry repeated the words rather scornfully. "I made that engine, Pop. I made it! And it works."

He turned the tap off again, and the engine ground to a halt. By now steam was pouring out of the leaky joints, and the machine did not look very impressive. But William knew that Henry was very proud of his achievement, and he did not want to hurt the boy. On the other hand, he felt that his son would be making a big mistake if he gave up his farming career.

"You've done a fine job, son," he said. "But, after all, is this going to get you anywhere? This is a prosperous farm, son. You'll get a good living from the land. We've done very well these last few years. And in the next few years we should do a lot better. So don't lose your heart to these machines. Machines never took the place of human work, son. The man who can plough and plant and reap the harvest—he's the man who will always make a living, no matter what may happen to the rest of the world."

Henry had heard this sort of remark so often that he took little notice. He had, after all, taught himself a lot about machines of many kinds. He could repair all sorts of things from ploughs to watches; he thought that, given a little more practical knowledge, he would be able to *make* all sorts of machines—maybe ranging from ploughs to watches. But he would not be able to do this while he remained in little Dearborn, and while he was tied to his father's farm. One day, he would have to break away. Just how he would be able to do this he could not tell. But sooner or later he would have to go and work in a place where machines were made. Looking after cows and pigs, planting all sorts of crops from corn to potatoes—these things were all very well in their way, and these things had made up his father's life for many years. Henry resolved that they should not make up *his* life. Sooner or later he would get to know more about machines.

It was a long time that night before Henry went to sleep. He was thrilled at the way in which his engine worked. Soon he would have to leave school. His father had taken it for granted that the boy would then become a full-time worker on the farm. How, Henry wondered, could he avoid that?

CHAPTER THREE

ON TO DETROIT

Soon Henry Ford left school. And soon there came what might have been a battle royal—the battle between Henry and his father. Henry made a stand. He wanted to work out his own life. His father had for so long assumed that Henry would help more and more on the farm, and would take over its management some time in the future, that it was a shock when the boy announced that he was not content to work things out in this way.

Henry was not bothered very much about the sort of job he would get if he moved to Detroit. In this large industrial town he was sure that there would be opportunities in plenty to learn about machinery—and to learn about machinery was his great ambition. He considered that the last few years, during which he had taught himself how to deal with machines of many kinds, had been very much worth-while. Yet, at the same time, he was sure that he had now reached the point when he should widen his experience. Self-tuition in engineering was all very well, but it had its limits, and Henry thought that he had reached those limits. He was now at the stage where he had to learn from other people. That there were many men in Detroit far more experienced and far more skilled than himself, he was certain. And to go and seek them out was the only way that he could see ahead. He knew that his father might well fight against this decision; but if so, he would have to fight back.

30

When Henry broke the news, William Ford was horrified.

"*Detroit?*" he said in amazed tones, frowning fiercely. "What on earth for? Why?"

"To get experience," Henry tried to explain.

"Can't you get all the experience you need here?" his father demanded.

"No, Father. Not experience of the right kind."

"And what is the right kind?"

Henry grinned. He thought he could see his way clear to win this argument with his father.

"Experience in an engineering workshop," he said. "I know quite a lot about machinery. But it's not enough—nowhere near enough."

"You could be a farmer, son," William Ford said. "A farmer is doing a better job than a mechanic—and he's doing a cleaner job too."

"I like machines, and I don't like farming," Henry said slowly. It was the first time he had ever dared to say as much to his father, and he was very doubtful about the way the news might be received.

"You're going away for good, then?" William Ford asked. "You'll stay in Detroit for good, and not come back to Dearborn?"

"I don't say that," Henry replied. "I expect I'll be back after a time. But I must go for a few months at least—maybe for a year or two—so that I can learn more about all sorts of machines and how they work."

"Don't you think you know enough about all the machines that you're ever likely to have to deal with?" his father asked him, still rather testily. "After all, you've been mending and fixing machines of every sort one can imagine for years past."

"That's true," admitted Henry. "But who can say what sorts of machines I might have to deal with some day? Farming may use more and more machines of many

31

different sorts before many years are past—and then it would be mighty useful to have someone about the place who knew how to mend them and fix them."

He was still by no means sure that he had really convinced his father; but—surprisingly enough—William Ford suddenly caved in and agreed.

"I won't stand in your way, Henry, if you think that, by going to Detroit to work, you can get some experience that will help you in the future."

"Thank you, Father," Henry replied. The battle had turned out to be not quite as fearsome as he had expected.

It was in the summer of 1880, when Henry was just about seventeen years old, that he set out for Detroit. All that he possessed was in one trunk, stowed at the back of a farm waggon. His father drove the waggon, with Henry sitting beside him. If William Ford felt any sort of deep emotion at the boy's leaving home, he did not show it. He may have had some doubts about Henry's chances of success in the big city; but perhaps he told himself, though he did not tell Henry, that it would not be long before the boy came home, and showed himself content with life on the farm in Dearborn.

Detroit was indeed a big city by nineteenth-century standards. It had a hundred thousand inhabitants, and thousands of those inhabitants worked in one branch or another of the engineering industry, for which the city of Detroit was widely famed. Henry had no doubt that, somewhere in that teeming mass of people, he would be able to find a little niche he could fill better than anyone else.

As it happened, the first place he tried for a job was looking for lively young men of Henry's type. James Flower & Brothers was a very good engineering firm, which made machinery of many kinds, though to some extent it specialized in the manufacture of small steam-engines. He had to work, as the foreman who engaged him pointed out, from seven o'clock in the morning until six o'clock at night. For that he would be paid the princely sum of two and a half dollars a week!

Henry had got this job before looking for somewhere to live. So he spent his first afternoon tramping around the city looking for a boarding house that was prepared to offer a room to a quiet and sober young apprentice on a wage of two and a half dollars a week. He saw some dirty places where he knew he would not be happy; and he soon decided that the cheapest boarding house that seemed to be in any way suitable would cost him more for his board and lodging than he was being paid for his work. Moreover, he had only five dollars in cash. By the time he had been in his job for a month his capital would be all spent.

However, he did not allow this to put him off. He paid his landlady a week's lodging in advance out of his precious five dollars. This left him less than two dollars in hand, but for the moment he did not allow this to upset him unduly. He was sure that he would be able to find a way of supplementing the small wage that his work as an engineering apprentice would bring him. He was happy because he was now to spend all his working hours among machines.

His first day was a little disconcerting, though. He had thought that, as an apprentice, he would at once be put on simple jobs with lathes and furnaces. He found that he was more like an errand boy than anything else.

"Boy! Bring me that piece of iron," one of the workers would say, indicating a huge and intimidating chunk of metal. Henry would somehow contrive to lift the heavy piece of iron on to a hand-truck, and would then trundle this truck across the workshop floor.

"This floor is filthy, Henry," someone else would say. "Get the broom and sweep it up."

This job was perhaps the most menial and the least interesting of all. "Hey, boy, bring me those chisels and that hammer," another man would shout, and Henry had to hurry across and fetch the necessary tools.

He had little chance to idle. But he thought to himself that if this went on for long, he would be gaining very little detailed knowledge of all the jobs that were being done—and he would be paying more for his lodgings than he was being paid for carrying out all these tasks.

He would certainly have to find something that would bring in a little extra money—and he would have to find it soon. His remaining cash would not last long.

So, as soon as he left work, he wandered around the streets, to try to discover something which would help to build up his scanty income. He soon spotted a watchmaker's shop, which was kept by a Mr. McGill.

Boldly Henry walked into the shop. Mr. McGill was seated behind the counter, with the parts of a watch he was repairing spread out before him on the table.

"I want a job," Henry explained. "I can repair watches. I've repaired a lot of watches in the last few years."

McGill smiled. "You don't look old enough to have spent years mending watches or doing anything else," he said. "And this is a bit late to be starting on a job."

Henry told him that he was an engineering apprentice, but that the job was not even well enough paid for him to cover the modest charge for his lodgings.

"Watch-mending pays no better than being an apprentice in a machine works," Mr. McGill said. "That's a pretty hard life too."

"It's hard all right," said Henry. "But I don't mind that. I want to go on with it, to get some experience of machines and how they are made. But I want to do some watch-mending too. I'll work at that in the evening."

"When do you want to start?" the watchmaker asked.

"I'll start right now, if you'll have me," replied Henry.

McGill was pleasantly surprised. He was so busy that he had been turning work away. It could be, if this young man was any good, that he would be a real help in the business.

"Sit you down over here, son," he said, making room at the counter. "That's a watch that I have just taken apart and cleaned and oiled. Let's see if you can put it together again. If you do that well, I'll offer you an evening job, all right."

Henry sat down, and spent a minute or two studying the parts of the watch that Mr. McGill had dismantled. He was glad to see that it was of a make with which he was already familiar. He had, indeed, repaired exactly the same kind of watch in his little shed across the farmyard at Dearborn. He looked at the tools available—little screw-drivers of far better quality than those with which he had been accustomed to work. Mr. McGill had been using a little eye-glass, such as many watchmakers had; Henry had never been able to afford one, but luckily his eyesight was sharp and he could see the tiniest parts of the watch without needing the magnification which the glass brought. So he started on the task of putting together the parts of the watch. In less than half an hour the task was complete, and the watch was ticking cheerfully on the table.

"Well done, son!" exclaimed Mr. McGill. "The job's yours."

"What hours do you want me to work?" asked Henry.

"Could you do four hours a night, six days a week?" asked McGill. He glanced at a clock above his head. "Could you get here at seven and work until eleven each night? I close my shop at eleven," he added by way of explanation.

"Start at seven tomorrow?" Henry asked.

"Yes."

"I'll be here," Henry agreed, as he made his way to the door.

"Hi! Wait a minute!" the watchmaker said. "Don't you want to know how much I'm going to pay you?"

Henry grinned. He had not thought of that. "How much can you pay?" he asked.

"Would two dollars a week make you happy?" asked the watchmaker.

"Suits me," Henry said, and strolled out of the shop, walking on air.

At one swoop he had solved his money problem. With two and a half dollars a week from James Flower & Brothers, and two dollars a week from Mr. McGill, he would have more than covered the cost of his board and lodging. His precious five dollars would soon be replaced, and even added to.

So there began what to most people would have seemed a terribly hard and thankless life. Henry got up at six o'clock each morning; he finished work at six o'clock at night, would eat a hasty snack meal, and be round at Mr. McGill's shop by seven. There he would happily work with the watches until eleven. Then he would go home to his lodgings, and fall asleep almost as soon as his head touched the pillow. At six the next morning he would jump out of bed, have a wash, and dress, to be at Flowers' by seven. Then the whole thing would start all over again. This went on for six days every week. Only on Sundays was there any break in the routine. To most boys it would have seemed incredibly dull and dismal; but Henry was learning about machines and their making, and this had been his ambition for so long that he was happy, even working such long hours. He was being paid, he would tell himself, to learn a job—and of how many people could that be said?

One Sunday he had a visitor. It was his father. William Ford had not really thought much of Henry's desire to become a mechanic or an engineer. Indeed, he had felt that it would not be many months before the boy came home to help on the farm. But he had received occasional letters in which there had been no hint of anything of the sort—so he decided to come into Detroit and have a chat with Henry.

He found that, in spite of the long hours which he was now working, Henry was quite happy. When he inquired if there was any likelihood of Henry's coming back to Dearborn, Henry told him that he did not think the time was yet ripe. He did not know enough about the machines he longed to understand.

"When spring comes," William said, "there will be a lot of work on the farm. I could do with your help then."

"A lot of hard work in the factory, too," Henry said with a smile. "Too much, in fact. There are a lot of heavy things that have to be shifted—things as heavy as the sacks of potatoes that you move about, Father."

"Isn't farm work easier, then?" William asked.

"I'm not sure," said Henry. "Carrying water by hand, for instance—that's hard work."

"But necessary. To listen to you, anyone would think that water could carry itself from the well to the horse and cattle troughs," William Ford replied with a loud laugh.

"And so it could."

"How?"

"Through pipes, like the water does here in the city," retorted Henry.

"Piped water on a farm!" his father exclaimed. "Who ever heard of that! Who would pay for the pipes? And how would you force the water through them?"

"You could have a pump, and you could have a steam-engine to drive it, you know," Henry said.

William Ford almost lost patience. This son of his was getting more and more foolish in his obsession with machinery. Now he wanted to use machinery to replace the human labour which had for centuries been used to do so many necessary jobs about the farm.

"So you are going to stay in Detroit for ever, son, just to have the pleasure of seeing water come out of a pipe

37

when you turn the tap!" he said. "The farmers will never be able to pay for that sort of stuff. It's all very well for city folk. But it will never come our way."

"One day it will," Henry replied emphatically. "I'll be back one day, Father, never worry, but that day won't be for a while yet. I don't know enough."

So William Ford made up his mind that he would not have his young son helping with all the routine tasks on the farm—not for a time yet, at any rate. It was a nuisance: he would have to pay an extra worker, instead of getting his son to work for him free of charge. That seemed to William Ford a wicked waste of money, and he was really hurt at the thought that a boy who was now tall and strong should be wasting his energies in a dirty factory and spending the evenings slaving away in a watchmaker's shop. Why, William asked himself, wasn't Henry content with repairing watches around Dearborn? That would have brought him in some money, and he could have done it at the time of the year when the work of the farm was at its lightest.

By now Henry was getting into his stride at the factory. Behind him were the days when he was just a kind of errand boy. There were others, now, who were junior to him, and who could be given the task of fetching tools or sweeping the workshop floor. At first Henry was given minor jobs, such as cutting iron bars or dividing metal plates. Soon, however, he graduated to using lathes and other important pieces of apparatus.

And then, after doing heavy industrial work all day, he would eat his hasty meal, and make his way to the watchmaker's shop, there to use tools as dainty and delicate as any that he had ever handled.

It was a very mixed life; and it was to stand him in good stead in the years ahead, when he was to do all sorts of tasks in the automobile industry.

He was not only engaged in practical work, either. He

learnt the basic theory of his trade. He haunted some of the bookshops, and bought a few books on engineering. He spent his spare money on journals and magazines. Unlike many of his mates, he never bought beer or tobacco. All his life Henry was to think that drinking and smoking were utterly wasteful, and that no one worth his salt ever spent hard-earned money on such things.

Henry loved his work. As he learned to work in metal, he was able to see how the many component parts were built together to form a massive machine, and this was what really fascinated him most of all. But he also saw that many wasteful things went on, and all this was stored in his mind, to come out again when the time arrived for him to plan his own factories. He was always critical of the way in which time and labour were wasted by an un-satisfactory workshop layout. He remembered his first days there when he had forever—or so it seemed—been running to take tools needed by some mechanic from one side of the shop to another. Why, he would ask himself, could not the tools lie ready to hand, so that when a man wanted a chisel or a hammer he would only have to stretch out his hand to pick it up? It was really just another variation on the waste of labour on the farm where water was carried by hand, bucket after bucket, from a well to a cattle trough, while a pipe would have done the job easily and well.

Henry did not say much about this to his factory-mates. He knew that such criticism would not appeal to them— and if it came to the ears of the management, it might well get Henry Ford into trouble. But as he went about his daily work, he weighed up all sorts of things in his mind, and decided how differently he would manage things if— or rather, when—he had the task of making the decisions.

It seemed to him that there was far too much moving about the workshop—both labour and materials—and far too little specialization. Everyone seemed to be expected to do everything. This was, of course, sensible for a young man learning something about the industry. But when a man was specially suited to one job, he should, Henry thought, be allowed to stick to that job only.

He was so good at the various jobs that were given him that he had now got a rise in pay. From two and a half dollars a week, he stepped up to three dollars—and he was still earning two dollars a week from his watch-repairing.

He was, however, beginning to think that he had learned all that he could from James Flower & Brothers. The rise of fifty cents a week which he had won did not mean much. He was not a grasping young man, eager to squeeze every cent possible out of his employer. He was aiming at getting experience. To get new experience he would have to change his job and start work with another firm.

That new firm was the Detroit Drydock Company. With them Henry stepped down from his newly-won three dollars a week, and went back to two and a half dollars a week. The foreman thought that Henry was crazy, to set out to cut his income by fifty cents a week—and just at a time when it seemed that he was set for rapid promotion in Flowers'. If he had stayed there, he might well have got more money as the months and the years passed by; but he would never have got beyond the stage of being a skilled mechanic. Though Henry Ford wished, quite early in life, to become a skilled mechanic, he wanted something else as well—he wanted to know enough about engines of all kinds to be able to design and make machines of his own. He probably knew, too, that even if he looked at the question simply from the point of view of cash return, the money which he would make by designing new machines would, in the end, be far more than he would ever make by working for James Flower or for any other firm.

The Detroit Drydock Company was much bigger than

James Flower & Brothers. It was also in some respects more specialized in that it made only marine engines. The fact that it specialized was the main reason why Henry had sought a job there. He had felt that James Flower & Brothers spread their energies over too many different projects of very different kinds, and he thought that to start work with a firm which made one form of engine, and one only, was more likely to give him the kind of experience which he would find valuable in the future.

He found, however, that specialization was not as much a royal road to success as he had thought. It was true that the Detroit Drydock Company made only one sort of engine—engines for boats. But they made so many different models of marine engine that in some ways they were little more specialized than James Flower had been. Still, Henry went on working for them, trying to learn as much about marine engines as he could meanwhile.

He also went on working for McGill, mending watches nearly every evening. His pay there continued at two dollars a week; and this enabled him to buy various engineering journals, as well as helping very considerably towards the cost of his lodgings. He had known quite a lot about watches during his later school years in Dearborn; but as he continued to work away at the back of McGill's shop, he found his knowledge deepening and broadening. Watches had, up to this time, been luxury goods because they were very expensive. One or two firms had now started to make cheaper watches, and as a result, more and more people were buying them. Sometimes a customer would come in to buy a new watch, and would leave an old one, more or less worn-out, contemptuously on the counter.

"What about your old watch?" McGill would ask. "Shall I wrap it up?"

"No," the customer would reply. "It's worn out. No use to me."

And if McGill did not want the watch, as he sometimes did for spare parts, Henry would get it. Then Henry would work on it in his spare time, and, as often as not, succeed in getting it to keep good time.

Over a year or two, in this way, Henry acquired as many as three hundred watches of different makes. A few of them were not usable; but most of them he had succeeded in getting to work.

It was at that time that he had an idea that might have got somewhere if he had pursued it a little further. He had seen that the gradual reductions in price had put watches within the reach of people who, a few years earlier, would never have thought of buying them. But most watches were still made largely by hand, which meant that there was a very real limit to the price reduction which could be aimed at.

Henry wondered if it would be possible to have a watch factory, in which the parts would be stamped out by machines. In his scanty spare time he made drawings of the parts that could be thus mass-produced. He had met a young jeweller in Detroit, and he used to talk to this young man by the hour, in the end infecting him with his own enthusiasm for the idea.

It would be possible, Henry said, to sell watches incredibly cheaply if they were made this way. He even suggested that, if enough of the parts could be die-stamped from sheet metal, it might be possible to get the price of a watch down to thirty cents.

There would have to be a fair amount of capital provided before such a watch factory could be started. The jeweller thought one or two of his wealthy customers might be persuaded to put up some money and back the scheme.

Then, for some reason, Henry abandoned the idea. He said, long after, that he had come to the conclusion that watches were not real necessities, and that, though he might produce them by the thousand, there would be no likelihood that thousands of people would buy them. A certain Mr. Ingersoll, not many years later, proved that this conclusion was faulty. But it is interesting to think that, if Henry had gone on with his watch-making scheme, it might have been Ford watches and not Ford cars which would have sold all around the world.

It should be noted, though, that the idea of making the parts cheaply by standardizing and die-stamping was central to Henry's ideal scheme. An idea not altogether unlike this was, before many years were over, to motivate him when he launched out truly in business for himself. But for the moment he went on working on marine engines all day, and on watches in his spare time.

CHAPTER FOUR

BACK TO THE FARM

His watch factory idea being abandoned, Henry contented himself with his work, both his main job and his spare-time work for the watch-maker. But he had not learned as much from the Drydock Company as he had hoped to begin with. Everyone who worked there was a kind of "Jack of all trades" and just as much time and labour was wasted in moving tools from one end of the workshop to the other. Henry felt in his bones that this was not the way in which a really efficient firm should be organized.

He therefore began to look around for a new job—if possible, one that would be somewhat better paid. To his joy a new post became available, and he applied for it. This was with the Westinghouse Company, which made road engines of the type Henry had seen years before when travelling with his father from Dearborn to Detroit. Henry had always been fascinated with these engines, and he was delighted that he would now have something directly to do with them.

He was not to assist in building them, however. He was to help to sell them, as an assistant to one of their leading salesmen.

The Westinghouse road engine at this time was, like the one Henry had seen as a schoolboy, really a stationary engine which was mounted on a waggon and harnessed to the back wheels by means of a big belt. It was not really intended to haul anything but itself. A few people used a Westinghouse engine to do haulage work, rather like a tractor. But it was not very efficient at this, and Henry, though he succeeded in selling a few, was not really very interested in them.

This engine was expensive and it was very heavy. It crawled around the roads to work a sawmill or a threshing machine. Though Henry persisted for a time in trying to push it into more general use he knew that its prospects were not promising. He was sure that the future of road transport did not lie with such an awkward and clumsy machine.

Henry began, indeed, to wonder if he had not made a mistake in coming to Detroit, though he had learned much about many different engines. He had saved a little money, and he thought that it might not be at all a bad idea if he spent this money on equipping himself as a mechanic, and then went home and helped with the repair and servicing of farm machinery in the area around Dearborn. He was, after all, still well known there, and though "the Ford boy" was now a young man, he was much better equipped to do all kinds of repairs.

Henry therefore bought himself a proper forge, to replace the rather primitive home-made one which he had previously owned, a far better lathe than any he had previously had at his disposal, and a variety of tools. With all this equipment, he thought, he would be able to make a living as a mechanic. So he set off for home.

William Ford had not been told that Henry was going to come back. But when he saw his son strolling across the farmyard the older man's face was wreathed in smiles. At last! The prodigal son had come home again, William Ford told himself. But he had to admit that, unlike the young man in the parable, Henry had not wasted his days in the great city, but had taught himself many useful things.

"I knew it wouldn't be long before you'd be back, son," William Ford said.

"Yes, here I am," said Henry. He knew in his heart, however, that he was not going to be quite the meek and mild son, obeying all the orders, that his father had hoped for. Henry had many ideas of his own, though it was to be some time before William was to get to know anything of them.

Yet—at any rate to begin with—Henry became a willing worker on the farm. He got up early to do the milking, he collected eggs from the hens, he fed the pigs and horses. He did not really like the routine work of the farm any more than he had done before going to Detroit; but he knew that as long as he lived there, he would have to help in the tasks that needed doing day by day.

He extended the shed in which he had worked long ago, and made it a much more useful workshop. In it he put all the new equipment that he had brought home from Detroit. He looked over the tools and other things that were in use on the farm, and was not altogether surprised to see that they had been neglected, and were no longer in as good condition as they had been.

The home was run by Henry's sister Margaret. She was a pretty girl, and she was glad to organize all sorts of social events. In the autumn, when the harvest had been gathered in, the Ford farmhouse was the centre of a thanksgiving supper and dance. Margaret sent out invitations far and wide, and a crowd of young people met in a big barn for this cheerful evening.

Henry enjoyed the supper, but was not very interested in dancing, which he thought was pretty much of a waste of time. His sister tried to persuade him that it would be a good thing for him to learn to dance; but to begin with he was not convinced.

At this first grand supper and dance he was very much struck by Clara Bryant, the young daughter of a neighbouring farmer from Greenfield, not far from Dearborn. To Henry's chagrin Clara was so much in demand as a

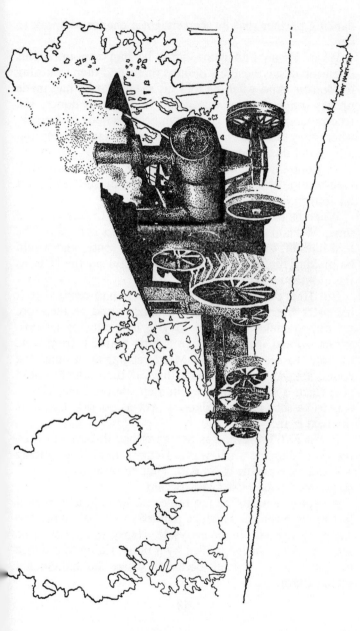

A steam engine of the type being built when Henry Ford was a young man

dancing partner that he scarcely got a chance to speak to her.

When Henry had come home he had announced his intention of having a few months there, and then returning to Detroit. And when he told his sister that he had made up his mind that he was going to learn to dance, she recommended him to go to a dancing school in Detroit, where they guaranteed to teach any novice to be a reasonably good dancer in only a few lessons.

"I guess I'll not be going back to Detroit for a while," Henry said. "I'll stay at home and help on the farm for a bit longer yet."

When he told his father that he planned to stay on for a time, William Ford beamed from ear to ear. Now, he told himself, this son of his had learned sense, and would be making himself more and more useful on the farm as the months rolled by.

But Henry's ideas were different. He had realized that his sister Margaret was a good dancer, and he therefore set out to make her agree to give him dancing lessons. William Ford was more than a little amused, from time to time, to see Henry and Margaret jigging around the room, singing together a rhythmical tune which would give them a chance to keep in step. Before long, Henry was to be seen at many dances, now as good a dancer as the next man.

It was not, however—as Margaret had discovered—just the joy of dancing which was in Henry's mind. The dancing was only the means to an end. That end was to get better acquainted with Miss Clara Bryant.

As another means to the same end he built a sledge—a fast-moving vehicle which he painted bright red. When the snow lay deep in the countryside, Henry was often to be seen in his red sledge, pulled by a pony, riding to a dance or some other special occasion where he anticipated seeing Clara.

He had succeeded in getting her to dance with him. But he did not, to begin with, know if he had made any sort of real impression on her. She was a pretty and popular girl, and she was always surrounded by a crowd of young men. She had more dancing partners than she could accommodate, and if she were given up by one young man at the end of a dance, there was usually a queue waiting to take his place.

Yet Henry was more and more impressed with Clara. And one day he got his father alone in front of the fire, and told him what was in his mind.

"Father," he said, "I want to marry Clara Bryant."

"Have you asked her?" William Ford enquired.

"Not yet."

"Well, before you do, ask yourself what you have to offer her," said his father.

"I can offer her myself."

William Ford grinned. "A very good offer, too, son," he said. "But I didn't mean that. I meant that you should be able to tell her something of how you will be able to keep her if she marries you."

Henry had great confidence in himself. He was sure that he would be able to earn enough to keep a wife as well as himself. But Mr. Ford thought that sheer confidence was not enough. Henry would have to have some tangible proof to show Clara that he had made good in the world and that if she married him, she would not find it too difficult to make ends meet in the home.

Eventually William Ford made the young man a good offer. He would give Henry forty acres of the good farmland. Part of it was already planted with corn and vegetables, and these crops would bring in an income over the next few months. The remainder was still rather rough tree-clad slope. If Henry was prepared to put his back into the work, he would be able to cut down a lot of the trees. Some of the resulting timber he would be able to sell; the rest would be enough to build a house in which he and his bride (if he succeeded in winning her) could live.

So now Henry had plenty to do. He soon set about getting the trees felled, and engaged a man to help with the actual building. Meanwhile he got on with what was perhaps an even more difficult task—persuading Clara to marry him. He was not a fast worker in his courtship. Indeed, it was a good two years before his house was finished. Not until then did he actually propose marriage to Clara. But before he asked, he was fairly certain what her answer would be.

It was in April, 1888, that they were married. They did not have a honeymoon, but Henry brought his bride proudly home to the house that he had helped to build. Soon they had settled into the timber house, made from trees on the farm, and Clara, who came from a farm herself, became a typical American farmer's wife of the time.

Henry went on with all his work on machines of one sort and another. He had fitted up a portable sawmill; when neighbouring farmers were nearly breaking their backs sawing up tree-trunks, Henry simply got his sawmill working. In the end, too, he rigged up a little crane, with a series of ropes, to lift the logs into position, so saving himself another energy-wasting chore. At times when the routine work of the farm was well under control, he would do some sawing for nearby farmers. This was work which was well-paid, and so Henry found his income slowly climbing up.

He also did some buying and selling of cattle. He had a shrewd business brain, and only on very rare occasions did he fail to make a profit. He managed to get appointed as the Dearborn agent of a firm making portable stationary engines, and sold a number of these, at a suitable profit, to farmers who wanted to ease the work of pumping water or sawing wood. The old part-time task of watch-repairing went on too. Before he knew where he was, Henry found his time so filled up that he could scarcely find an hour to read the engineering journals which came along to him week by week or month by month.

He soon found it an awful waste of time to walk from his own farm to his father's in order to use the engineering equipment which he had brought home with him from Detroit; so he built a new and bigger workshop on his own farm, and moved all his things from the old shed into the big and more convenient new one.

In the back of his mind there was still the thought of the self-propelled steam-engine that he had seen years before. He recalled, too, the Westinghouse engines that he had sold in the last few months before his return home. He was sure that he could, given the opportunity, make a better engine than those rather clumsy early models. And in the little spare time that was left over from his many tasks, he set out to see if he could design something better.

He had, of course, made a model engine years before. It had not been wholly satisfactory, though it had run across the farmyard. Now he set to work to create something better, and he had some success with small models, which were capable of a considerable turn of speed.

Then he tried to make a bigger engine. Now he found a very real snag, which had not previously occurred to him. When he made an engine big enough and powerful enough to provide the pulling-power that he was after, the boiler and the water in it were so heavy that the engine used nearly all its energy in pulling itself along.

He spent many months making a steam-car which ran fairly well and reached quite a good speed. It was heated not by coal but by oil-burners. The boiler was underneath the seat, to save space. However, this was not likely to be a very safe arrangement, Henry decided, when he had been out for one or two rides. He did not like the idea of being scalded by a hot boiler under the seat on which he was sitting.

The real trouble was that the roads of Michigan were rough. In his engineering magazines Henry read descriptions of some steam-driven cars that were in use in England. They seemed to work quite well. Henry thought, however, that English roads were almost certainly smoother than the rough roads of the United States. On smoother roads, a steam-car might be a practical proposition. On rougher roads it just did not have a chance. Some of the English engines were quite big. Yet Henry was sure that in America they would not be satisfactory. In the end he dropped the scheme, thinking that it was just a waste of time until the surface of the roads got better—and that might be a very long way ahead in time.

He wondered, sometimes, if some more satisfactory way of propelling an engine could be used—a way which would do away with the heavy boiler and the need to carry large quantities of water.

All this time he had been buying engineering journals and magazines, and he often glanced through them to see if there were any suggestions about other possible ways of harnessing power, so that a vehicle might be built which would drive itself along the roads.

There was, for example, a German inventor called Otto. He produced a car that would run, with coal-gas as its propelling agent. This had many flaws—for one thing, using gas meant that very bulky bags had to be carried as containers. Another was that there was always some danger of a leak. And a coal-gas leak would cause an explosion.

So the Otto gas engine was not satisfactory. But Henry recalled that in a works at Detroit there had been a not dissimilar engine which ran, not on coal-gas, but on the vapour from petrol—the liquid that Americans were coming to call "gasoline". This engine had not been altogether satisfactory either, but Henry had been called in to look at it and had managed to make it work. But he thought that he would one day be able to make a better engine of his own.

After he had come to decide that steam-engines were not very practical means of getting along the rough roads of nineteenth-century America, Henry remembered this petrol engine.

He had a fair idea of the way in which it had worked, and he decided that he would try to make a model one. He worked on a very small scale. The cylinder in which the piston moved was only about an inch (25 mm) in diameter, and the piston moved up and down only three inches (75 mm). But it showed that the idea was workable. The machine, like most of Henry Ford's machines, was a satisfactory working device. Whether it would be as satisfactory if made on a far bigger scale was doubtful, but Henry decided that one of these days, when he had a little more time to spare than the work on the farm allowed, he would try to construct a full-scale working petrol-driven engine. For one thing, the weight of such an engine would be much less than that of the steam-engines with which Henry had been working ever since coming back to Dearborn.

He was now becoming more and more useful to his father on the farm. Henry had developed into a tall, muscular man; and William Ford much appreciated the fact that he had his son at home to help with many of the harder tasks farm life involved.

Yet, in spite of all the weekly chores on the farm, Henry still kept his keen interest in machines alive. He read widely in the engineering magazines and journals. But it was not only theory that he studied. When his father sent him, as he often did, to the big cattle-markets in Detroit, he would get the work done first, selling the cattle—and Henry would usually manage to sell them at a good price, for he was always a good business man; this over, he would wander into the part of the big city where engineering of one kind or another was carried on, and go into any factory which was working.

"What do you want, young man?" a foreman in an engineering shop would ask him on such occasions.

"Just to look," Henry would reply with a friendly grin.

"Just to look at what?"

"To look at the machines," Henry would say, and would then wander along the workshop floor, peering at one machine after another, trying to see what job it was designed to do, and how well it was doing it.

There were occasions when he was chased off by some angry owner, who thought that he was a kind of spy, endeavouring to steal details of some secret process. More often, however, he would succeed in finding a fellow-enthusiast somewhere in the factory, and then he would be able to talk about machines to his heart's content.

Clara was not altogether alarmed at her husband's tendency to linger in Detroit. She was not yet able to understand his great keenness to learn about machines; but soon after they were married she had come to see that her husband was a very remarkable man, very different from the rank and file of farm workers in the district.

"We shan't always go on like this, Clara," he said one evening.

"Like what, Henry?" she asked.

"We shan't be struggling and doing back-breaking jobs day after day, week after week. We shall get machines to do the jobs for us. That will be the way out."

"Yes, Henry," his wife answered almost meekly. She had been born on a farm, and had lived on one all her life. She had never imagined that the old way of running a farm could change. But if it did happen, she knew that it would be a man like her husband who would have most to do with bringing the change about.

Then, one day in 1891, when he had been back in Dearborn for over two years, Henry went into Detroit and stayed much longer than he had ever done before. He left home early in the morning, and did not get back until nearly midnight. His wife had been very worried about him. She had visions of Henry being knocked down and robbed in the big city.

When she heard him opening the front door she rushed to him.

"Wherever have you been all this time, Henry?" she asked. "I've been mighty worried about you."

Henry smiled. "I'm sorry if you were worried, Clara," he said. "But I couldn't let you know what was happening until it actually happened."

"And what did happen?" his wife inquired. "What kept you in Detroit all those hours?"

"We're going to live in Detroit soon, Clara," he said slowly.

"Yes, Henry?" There was a questioning tone in her voice, though she did not ask the question in as many words.

"Yes, Clara," he said. "I've been offered a job with the Edison Illuminating Company."

"Is it a good job?"

"*I* think it is."

"How much are they going to pay you?"

"Forty-five dollars a month," Henry said.

"Forty-five dollars a month! That's more than you're making out of your farming, Henry."

"Yes, it is. But of course the work that I put into the farm helps to improve the land and make it more valuable. But even so, I've not accepted that job in Detroit mainly for the money. I've accepted it because it will give a better chance to work out my new machines."

Clara Ford accepted the idea of moving to Detroit without too much opposition. Henry was certain enough, however, that his father would look at the idea in a very different way.

The next morning, though, Henry took his courage in both hands and went to his father, in order to explain why it was that, after a little over two years in the new farming set-up, he was now planning to go back to Detroit, and back to the routine of the engineering workshop—so very different from the routine of the farm.

"You're a fool, Henry Ford!" his father said, as soon as Henry had provided an outline of what it was that he was proposing to do.

"Why do you say that?" Henry asked. "I think that this new job of mine is a job that looks into the future."

"In farming there's no job that goes peering into the future," William Ford said. "Farms have always been run in one way, and in that one way they will go on. That way is the way of good hard slogging work."

"There's no virtue in good hard slogging work, Father," Henry pointed out. "At least, there's no virtue in it if you can make a machine to do the work more cheaply and more quickly."

"You've been working about fifteen hours a day on the farm," William Ford said. "You've been making how much profit? Twenty dollars a month? Twenty-five?"

"Thirty dollars a month, as near as I can calculate," Henry admitted.

"Thirty dollars a month profit. And the farm improving all the time, so that soon—in a year or two, anyhow—you'd be making thirty-five or forty dollars a month."

"Oh, I know you're right," Henry said. "But I want to go to Detroit."

"How much will this blamed engineering company pay you?" asked his father. "After all, you should be making enough to offset your giving up a good thirty dollars a month profit on the farm. What are they going to pay you? How much a month?"

"Forty-five dollars," Henry said. He had thought that this would take some of the wind out of his father's sails, but not a bit of it! His father was quite prepared to go on arguing, to compare the cost of living in Detroit with the cost in Dearborn, to point out that, when he was on the farm, Henry could get milk and eggs and butter and vegetables for next to nothing, whereas in the great city he would have to pay for all these things. And William Ford went back to an old argument which he had used years before. It was the argument about the danger to health of working in a big, smoky city. The countryside, he said, was so much healthier to live in.

No matter what Henry might say, his father did not budge in his opposition. Of course, William Ford could do little about it in any practical sense, because his son was now nearly thirty years of age and very much his own master. Yet William still grumbled endlessly, as Henry and Clara set about tidying up their affairs and making themselves ready to go into Detroit as soon as might be.

CHAPTER FIVE

AT WORK AND IN LEISURE

There can be little doubt that Henry's real desire in coming to Detroit was not simply to work for the Edison Illuminating Company. It was probably true to say that this famous company provided him with the means toward an end. And that end was his old, old ambition of building a road-engine—a "horseless carriage", as some enterprising journalists called it.

Although Henry appeared to have proved to his own satisfaction, if not to everyone else's, that steam traction engines were not practicable for running on ordinary roads in the United States, he still had not given up the idea of a self-propelled vehicle of some sort.

It was at first very mysterious to his wife. To begin with, Clara just found it impossible to understand what he was getting at. Gradually, however, Henry infected her with his own enthusiasms. It was said that when many other people laughed at his ideas of a horseless carriage, he would refer to his wife as "the believer", saying that she was the only person in the world who really believed in what he was trying to do.

Henry found the Edison Illuminating Company fairly hard task-masters. He had, however, known before starting with them, what would be likely to be expected of him. He started work in the factory at six o'clock in the morning, and, with very short meal-breaks, was kept busy until six o'clock at night. A twelve-hour day at work would have been enough for most people. But when

Henry got home, he fairly gobbled down the meal that his wife had prepared, and then made his way out to a shed at the back of the little house that he had rented in Detroit. His wife may have felt, on occasion, that he did not take much notice of the meals which she cooked with such great care. Yet she knew that he was so absorbed in his work that he could not pay very much attention to the food that he was eating.

The Edison firm was largely concerned with making electric motors and other machines concerned with the rapidly growing electricity industry. Much of the factory was, however, run on steam power. At first, when he started there, Henry was concerned with the various steam-engines which were in use. He was by now something of an expert on such engines, and if one broke down he was soon able to get it working again.

His employers were very pleased with what he was doing. When he had been at work there for only a matter of two or three months, he came home one evening in a state of great excitement, his face fairly beaming with joy.

"You look very pleased with yourself tonight," his wife said, as she took his hat and coat from him, and hung them up.

"I *am* very pleased with myself," Henry said.

"Why? What's happened?"

"I've got a raise."

"More pay?"

"Yes."

"How much are they going to pay you?" Mrs. Ford asked.

"Guess," challenged Henry, a rare and unusual twinkle in his eye.

"Fifty dollars a month?"

"More."

"Fifty-five dollars a month?"

"More."

Clara Ford stamped her little foot on the floor in an impatient way. "How dare you tease me like this?" she asked. "How much are they going to pay you?"

"Seventy-five dollars a month," Henry said.

It was, indeed, a sign of the fine work that Henry had been doing for the Edison Company that they soon doubled his starting pay. Within nine months of his starting work there he was earning a hundred dollars a month, and shortly afterwards this went up to a hundred and twenty-five dollars. By this time he was chief engineer at the factory.

It was a fine job for a young man. But it was a job that brought him much hard work and very long hours. He was twelve hours a day in the factory, supervising all the work of the place. And when he got home he was still "on call", like a doctor, liable to be roused at any time if a machine went wrong and his expert attention was needed. He had no deputy; he could not go on holiday, for there was no one to take his place. Just what would have happened if he had been taken seriously ill it was impossible to say—he wondered about this sometimes. But fortunately he was a very healthy man, and no illness struck him down in those early days.

And still he worked away in that little workshop between hours. He would start straight after his evening meal, and work on until bed-time—and very often bed-time was somewhere in the early hours of the morning. Mrs. Ford got used to spending periods of time alone. Sometimes, if she felt too lonely, she would go out to the workshop and watch him, though often she did not really appreciate what he was doing.

She sometimes got worried about this tireless husband of hers. She was sure that it was not good for him to spend so long at the factory, and then, on his return home, to work so long there. There were, indeed, some occasions when he would work almost all through the night, snatching only an hour or two of sleep before it was time to get up again and set off for his regular job at the works.

The idea that filled his mind, in those long hours in his little shed-workshop, was the idea of a horseless carriage. He had, as has already been said, come to the conclusion that a steam vehicle was just not practicable in American conditions; but what could replace steam as a propelling power? He had read a little about experimental cars which were being built in Europe. In Britain there was a law that if a mechanical vehicle ran along the road, it had to be preceded by a man on foot, carrying a red lantern at night and a red flag in daylight. In spite of this discouraging attitude on the part of the authorities, there *were* people in Britain who were trying to design engines which would propel a car along a road. And on the continent of Europe there were more—Daimler, Benz, Bouton, Panhard and others whose names were later to become household words, were thinking their way through to the building of a practical machine. In England a young man called Royce was trying to work things out in a similar fashion.

Henry Ford, thousands of miles away from these pioneers, got only very occasional news of what they were trying to do. Since most of their experiments were intended to lead to great profits, little appeared about them in the papers and magazines. And in any case most of the papers and magazines that came Henry's way were American ones; and in those days news from Europe took longer to find its way to the USA, and Americans were far less interested in engineering progress in Europe than they were to become in the twentieth century.

The result was that Henry, though he might get some idea of what was going on across the Atlantic, was to a large extent probing in the dark in his efforts to build a car of his own. He knew that other people were working on more or less parallel lines; but he had very little detailed knowledge of just what they were doing. Yet he knew the principle on which the "internal combustion engine" worked, and he knew that eventually such an engine would replace the clumsy and dirty steam-powered affair which had previously been used.

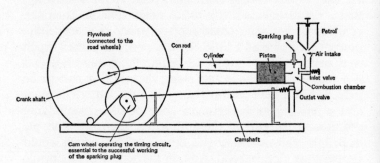

This diagram illustrates, in simplified terms, the principle on which an internal combustion engine operates. A four-stroke cycle begins with the piston at the top of its stroke. The inlet valve is open, and on its first downstroke the piston sucks a mixture of petrol mist and air into the cylinder. The inlet valve closes, and the piston is pushed up again (by the revolving of the crankshaft), compressing the air/vapour mixture into the combustion chamber. A spark passes between the metal points of the sparking plug. The air/vapour mixture is ignited and the piston is forced down on its second downstroke. At the end of the downstroke, the outlet valve opens, and during the second upstroke, the burnt gases are pushed out of the engine. The correct timing of the opening and shutting of the valves is controlled by the camshaft

The cylinder in an internal combustion engine contained a combustion chamber in which a mixture of air and vapour was exploded by a spark. The vapour came from a very volatile oil which was called petrol in Great Britain and gasoline (commonly "gas") in the United States. It was fairly easy to get, and was not unduly expensive to buy. The real problem, as Henry had found with small models, was to control the spark which exploded the air-vapour mixture. This explosion pushed the piston along the cylinder. To harness the piston so that its regular movements to and fro, thrust forward by the regular small explosions in the combustion chamber, would push the car along was not a difficult problem—Henry had, indeed, solved it already in his experimental steam cars. But how to make and break the spark at timed intervals, so that the piston would be thrust forward and the wheels would turn and the vehicle would move—that was the most difficult problem to solve.

Henry also thought that the body of his car would have to be kept as light as possible. A heavy carriage would be that much more difficult to keep moving; and if his car were to carry passengers or goods, he must not waste a lot of the motive-power simply in pushing the vehicle itself along.

It was the first petrol-driven car that Henry was building in those early days at the back of the house in Bagley Avenue, Detroit. His neighbours thought he was crazy, when they thought about him at all. Mrs. Ford's friends were deeply sympathetic, for her husband never seemed to take her out for an evening's entertainment, or out for a drive in the country with a pony and trap at the weekend. Every moment that he could spare was spent in building his car.

Strange noises came from the shed—the noise of hammering, the hiss of hot steel being plunged into cold water, the buzz of the lathe, the smooth strokes of a plane cutting into wood or metal.

"Your husband still on with his machine?" a neighbouring housewife would ask quietly. "My husband is taking me out for a little trip into the country this weekend."

"Henry knows what he's doing," Mrs. Ford would reply.

"Maybe he does. But it's hard on you," the neighbour would comment.

"I'm quite happy. I know that what he's doing will get him somewhere in the end."

"In the end!" the neighbour would snort. "By the time he gets somewhere you'll be too old to enjoy yourself. He may make a million dollars in the end; but what's the good of a million dollars if you're rheumaticky and deaf?"

Mrs. Ford did not tell Henry of these comments from the neighbours. She knew that they would only upset him. She knew, too, that nothing, now, would deflect him from his ambition.

Henry sometimes heard some echo of the sarcastic remarks that were passed about him. It worried him that people might feel he was not in any way concerned about his wife's happiness. He loved her deeply, and one of the motives behind his great ambition was that if he made more money it would enable him to give her greater comfort. He was quite sure, in his own mind, that he would in the end be able to build a car cheaper than those built by anyone else, and that it would thus sell in large numbers and make him a very rich man indeed.

Meanwhile, he just had to plug on, trying to build the first car of his particular sort.

Of course, he was embarking on what was to all intents and purposes a new field. He could not just go along to some firm of engineers and ask them to make some of the components for his car. He had to make all the parts himself in his workshop. Even the sparking-plugs which were to set off the little explosions in the cylinder—these had to be painfully made by hand. And these gave him most trouble of all, for he had to make an electric spark pass between metal points. This was a skilled and difficult job.

The wheels were second-hand wheels from a couple of

old tricycles which Henry picked up cheaply. The wheel hubs were old pieces of gas pipe. The cylinders were made from an old steam-engine which he bought from a dealer in junk. Everything he put into his car was second-hand and had originally been intended for some other use. It was no wonder that he had a long and worrying time putting it together, for every part meant hours and hours of laborious struggle.

When he had built his engine, he tried it out on a bench. It worked, though it made a terrible rattling noise, and the fumes it emitted smelled horrible.

But Henry had thought it out carefully. The engine had two cylinders, the diameter of each being half an inch (12·5 mm), and the piston stroke about six inches (150 mm). The engine developed four horse-power, and was mounted at the back of the car. Under the driver's seat there was a small tank which would hold three gallons (about 13 litres) of petrol, so placed that the fuel poured by gravity to the engine, where a valve mixed the petrol vapour with air.

The engine was at first designed to keep cool by air intake; but Henry soon found that it was liable to overheat pretty badly, so he put a water jacket around it and worked out a system to make the water circulate around the hot cylinders. This was, in fact, his first effort at making the cooling device which in future years was to become the radiator, a familiar feature of most cars.

Gears were almost non-existent, though Henry knew that he must introduce some kind of gearbox, so that the engine would operate at a higher speed when more power was needed and slow down to a lower speed when less power was needed. This would reduce the engine noise. In the end Henry worked out a system for a two-speed engine linked to the wheels by a belt. There was a lever alongside the driver's seat which was attached to the belt. The car ran fast when the lever was pushed in one position and slow when it was pushed in the other. In effect it was a two-geared car, with a set of cogs of various sizes to regulate its running to two speeds.

The first trials of the engine on the bench were fairly satisfactory, though Henry was not happy until it had run for some hours. This meant sundry alterations in design.

For months he tinkered about with it. Sometimes he would tell his wife what he felt to be wrong. And, even though she had no engineering knowledge, she would wrinkle her brows in bewilderment and see what she could understand—not always very much. But it was enough for her to know that he was getting somewhere, even though progress might be slow.

It was in 1892 that Henry was satisfied with his first petrol-driven car. First he got it out of the shed where it had been built, and into the yard. Here he started up the engine and ran it a short distance. He did not want to risk taking it on to the road until he was quite sure that it would not break down outside the front door. It had no reverse gear; so as soon as he had run it along the yard, he would stop the engine and painfully push the car back into the shed again. The whole process was still a frustrating business.

One day a neighbour looked at him over the fence. He sneered at Henry's painful pushing.

"It'll never work, Mr. Ford," he said.

"Wait and see," answered Henry shortly.

"I shall have to wait a long time, I guess."

Henry just grinned.

Then the neighbour made a remark which has been many times repeated. "If God had intended Man to go on wheels," he said, "he'd have put wheels on us, instead of legs and feet."

Henry was not unduly worried by such comments. He knew, now, that he was within striking distance of complete success. And, while there were still alterations that he would have to make, he knew that in a matter of months he would be driving the first Ford car down the street.

He was, of course, still working as chief engineer in the works. He was still called out to repair faulty machines, even when he was officially off-duty. So the time that he could spend in building his car was very strictly limited.

There was also a complication at home: his son was born in 1893. Named Edsel, this boy was the joy of Clara Ford's heart; and it meant that she was now absorbed in her baby, and was not able to spend so much of her time watching what Henry was doing and offering her comments and suggestions.

It was at about this time, too, that the car had its first trial run. Henry decided that he would not venture out on the street during the day, when there might be a lot of curious sightseers. He therefore set out at night. First he had to operate the cranking handle to get the engine started. This was before Edsel's birth, and Mrs. Ford was standing by to see what happened. As the engine started, Henry clambered into the seat and drove off. There was a lot of noise, and Mrs. Ford, trotting alongside the car, was amused to see lights going on in neighbouring houses, windows opening, and heads emerging to see what was happening. The coughs and noises of the engine were enough to arouse the curiosity of all but the soundest sleepers.

Henry drove the car some way along the street, turned around and came back. Then he ran the car into the yard behind his own house, and back into the shed, where he triumphantly brought it to a standstill.

"There, Clara! What do you think of that?" he said, as he made his way indoors.

"It runs, Henry," she said.

"Yes. It'll take a bit of fixing yet," he said. "There are a heap of things about it that will have to be improved. Still, it goes—and that is the main thing at the moment."

"What are you going to do now?" asked his wife.

"I'm going to have a glass of milk," Henry said, with a cheerful grin. "And then I'm going to bed."

Long years afterwards, Henry had to give evidence in a lawsuit, and when he was asked what happened to this car, he said: "I ran it around for two or three years, and I sold it to Mr. C. Ainsley of Detroit."

Henry Ford in his first car, built by hand from bits and pieces of second-hand material: a petrol-driven, two-cylinder vehicle which represented months of work and years of patient experiment

It all sounds very simple; and maybe it was simple to Henry, looking back over a period of years. But at the time there was a lot to be done to that first experimental car.

After each run, Henry got some sort of idea for improving it. So back it would be put in the shed, and some new component made and fitted. Then out on to the street again, to try it out and see how the new part worked.

After the first run, however, Henry was no longer shy about driving in daylight. He was no longer worried by criticism or silly and sarcastic remarks. After all, though the car was far from the perfection at which he was aiming, it did move, and in the end was to reach the hitherto unheard-of speed of nearly twenty miles an hour.

There were many problems, not all of them connected with the design of the car or its engine. For one thing, Detroit was a big city and it had a lot of traffic—private citizens, intent upon their business, and vans and drays carrying the goods needed to keep the life of the city going. All of this carrier traffic was, of course, horse-drawn. And horses in those days were not used to noisy motor vehicles. Many a time a horse, scared by the noise and smell of the first Ford car, would career along the street, more or less out of the control of its driver. Some owners of horse-drawn vehicles threatened to take Henry to court and sue him for being a real public nuisance. The police, too, found Henry a bit of a problem. If he stopped and parked his car anywhere, a crowd would soon assemble. Mischievous boys would climb on to the seat and pull the levers. It was said that on one occasion a crowd of curious bystanders pushed the car for fifty yards or so along the road, trying to get it to start. So from that moment on, Henry took a lock and chain with him. If he had to leave his car for more than a few moments, he would lock it firmly to the nearest lamp-post.

The police, indeed, called to see him one day.

"That your car, Mr. Ford?" asked the policeman, pointing to the vehicle, which was standing in the yard.

"Yes."

"It's causing a nuisance on the street. It scares the horses, and it makes a crowd gather round it. That's obstruction, you know."

"Surely, if I make my own car, and drive it along the public highway, I'm entitled to do it. I pay my taxes like everybody else," Henry retorted.

"Not sure that we can't sue you for being a public nuisance," the policemen pointed out.

So Henry made his way around to see the mayor. He pointed out that this was an experimental car that he had made. He could only make it perfect, he explained, by running it on the street. He saw no reason why he should be stopped from doing this.

"Who said you could be stopped?" asked the mayor.

Henry told him of this visit that he had suffered from the police. "There will be hundreds—maybe thousands— of these cars on the streets within a few years," he said.

"You think so?" queried the mayor.

"I'm sure of it," Henry said confidently.

"Well, you may be right or you may be wrong," the mayor said. "But I guess you must be allowed to run it when and where you like, as long as you don't do any damage or hurt anybody."

"Will you let me have a licence, allowing me to drive when and where I like in Detroit?" asked Henry quietly.

"I sure will."

Then and there the mayor drew up a licence, entitling Henry Ford to drive a horseless carriage within the confines of the city of Detroit. It was the first licence of its kind to be issued in the United States of America.

Henry was making history. And he knew in his heart that this was indeed a historic document—the first of the many millions of licences to be issued in the years ahead.

He ventured out into the surrounding countryside sometimes, too. His licence only covered the city area, but he was fairly confident that there would be less trouble when he got out into the country. Even there he found the problem of the scared horses; but by now he had become accustomed to stopping the machine if there was any sign that a horse was becoming unduly frightened at the noise which the car was making.

As he said in his evidence in court, he ran this car for some two or three years, all the time trying to improve its design and its performance. When, in the end, Mr. Ainsley paid him two hundred dollars for it, Henry set out at once to spend the money on buying better materials with which to build a better car.

Could he build cars cheaply enough to sell them in hundreds—or even thousands? Bicycles had already achieved a mass market. There was a bicycle boom in the 1890s; and Henry was sure that if he could bring the price of his car down to a reasonable level, he would soon find a similar boom in the sale of motor-cars.

CHAPTER SIX

INDEPENDENCE

Up to this point, the career of Henry Ford was not very different from the career of many another man in industry, whether in the United States, or on the European side of the Atlantic. There was the same feeling towards something new, the same experiments. It was not unlike the work George Stephenson had done in the early days of railways. It was not unlike the work Henry's contemporary, Edison, had done on the first motion-picture camera and projector. It was not unlike the work of Rolls and Royce in Great Britain.

What made Ford different from all these other pioneers, however, was his feeling that it should be possible to produce a motor-car at a price which would be within the reach of the masses. Quite early in his life as an experimental engineer, Henry Ford was sure that a car should not be a pure luxury for a millionaire, but should be something that the ordinary man in the street would be able to afford. This was his aim in those early days in Detroit—to work out a cheap method of making a motor-car which would lower the price and bring it within the means of ordinary working folk.

It was in 1896 that the second car was built. It was not all that different from the first model; but the bodywork was such that the car was much lighter in weight, which meant that it would be cheaper to propel, and would not use up as much fuel.

Mrs. Ford, now with little Edsel to look after, could not

spare as much time to see what her husband was doing. But he would talk at great length about the general improvements in design which he was now thinking out and applying. She listened with interest; but her ears were more often open to the possible cries of the baby in the little bedroom above.

Henry read the papers—the ordinary newspapers of the day, and the engineering journals, both American and European. He realized from all the reports that appeared that there were a number of people who were now producing cars which would run even on the rough-surfaced roads of the United States. But more and more he came to see that these cars were designed for a small public that could afford luxuries. The idea that the automobile could one day become the vehicle of the masses did not seem to have entered the minds of any of his rival inventors.

There was, too, the matter of weight. Henry had seen a Benz car from Germany, which was being shown off in New York. It ran quite well and smoothly; but it was expensive, and it was much heavier than the cars which Henry had already built. It was true that it had little niceties in construction which the Ford car had not—but there were still, in Henry's eyes, a number of real drawbacks which the designers of the Benz car did not appear to have thought about. Indeed, it appeared to Henry that all the cars which were brought across the Atlantic from Europe were far too heavy. They might, he thought, be designed to run on roads in Europe; but American roads were different, and he did not think that they would be at all satisfactory there.

Then, one day, the head of the Edison Illuminating Company of Detroit, of which Henry was still chief engineer, sent for Henry.

"They tell me that you are building automobiles?" he asked.

"That's right," Henry said.

"What drives them?"

"Petrol engines," Henry said.

"Petrol? Gasoline?"

"Yes."

"Waste of effort," said his chief.

"You think so?" Henry retorted.

"I do. Petrol's no good for that sort of thing. Electricity is the force of the future. Build an electrically-propelled car. We might take that up in a big way," said the head of the firm.

Henry smiled, making no comment. Then he went home and continued to work on his latest petrol engine.

Henry Ford was sure that an electrically-propelled car, while it might be satisfactory for short distances, would not be good enough for long runs. And the batteries which would be needed would be so heavy that a lot of the power would be wasted. A petrol engine would, he was sure, be so much lighter that it would be far cheaper in cost per mile of running.

It was during the year 1896 that Henry was sent to a conference of engineers from many factories from all over the United States. It was here that Henry met the great Edison himself. Another delegate at the conference introduced Henry to Edison, and told the great inventor that young Ford had built a petrol-propelled car. Edison was very interested, and when Henry described the sparking-plugs which he had designed, he was very impressed. Henry was then only a little over thirty years of age, and Edison was nearly fifty; but the older man was much impressed by the genius of Henry Ford. He commended Henry for what he was doing, and told him that he thought he was on the right track.

It was broad-minded of Edison, who had done so much with electricity, to see that there were many limitations on its use. He realised, as Henry had done, that the batteries to drive an electric car would be too heavy to be practicable. He saw, too, that the distance electric cars could cover would be very restricted, in that they would have to stay within reach of a major power station where the batteries could be re-charged when this became necessary.

Encouraged by Edison's interest, Henry went back to Detroit and started on his third car, which was again an improvement in some details over the second one. He was still completely dependent on his own labour and the help of one or two friends for the making of all the components, and he knew that, before he was able to bring down the price—this was his aim—he would have to find a way of making the bits and pieces far more cheaply. This, he knew, would mean that instead of the components being made painfully and individually by hand, they would need to be made in large numbers by some kind of machinery.

Meanwhile, unknown to Henry Ford, a patent was registered which was to cause endless trouble to the Ford family in the years ahead. In those days the patent laws in the United States were such that it was possible to patent something without going into the amount of detail later laws demanded. And the patent applied for by a lawyer called George B. Selden was as vague as could be. It specified "a safe, simple and cheap road locomotive". Mr. Selden thought that his patent covered pretty well any car that might be produced, and some of the firms then producing luxury cars in small numbers were prepared to pay him a certain amount of money so that there should be no danger of their infringing his patent. Henry may have heard of the Selden patent, though this appears doubtful. In any case he was not in any way conscious that what he was doing might be infringing the rights which Selden had established for himself.

Moreover, Henry was now offered a great advancement by his firm. In the years from 1896 to 1899, he had made himself more and more useful in his work. His chief, even though he thought that Henry was wasting his energy messing about with petrol engines, was well aware of his genius for electrical work, and Henry was offered the position of works superintendent. This would have meant a very considerable increase in pay. It would, too, have meant that the young man was now the head of a prosperous factory, It was very tempting. But it was quite clear to Henry that if he took this on, it would mean much added responsibility. It would almost certainly mean that he would have little, if any, time to spend on tinkering about with petrol engines. He was, in effect, being asked to choose between his car and the factory. The decision was a very difficult one, and for a time Henry hesitated.

"What do you think?" he asked his wife one evening, as they sat before the fire. "Should I take it?"

"You do what you feel best, Henry," she replied.

"There's a lot more security in being superintendent of the whole plant," he explained. "To spend my time building engines is a bit of a gamble, you know."

"Do what you feel best," said Mrs. Ford for the second time.

In a book he wrote long afterwards, Henry said: "I had to choose between my job and my automobile. I chose the automobile."

In August, 1899, therefore, Henry walked for the last time through the gates of the Illuminating Company. He was a free man! He was no longer tied down to factory hours. He was no longer called back to the works when some engine went wrong. But—also—he was no longer receiving a regular income. To make a living, to maintain himself and his wife and his growing son—this was up to him from now on. As he had said to his wife, it was a gamble, and Henry Ford was not naturally a gambler. But he wanted to build cars; he knew that he had it in him to build cars. The only way in which he could devote himself to building cars was to resign his job at the works.

He had very little capital; and the motor-car business

was, in those days, a very risky affair. In the whole of the vast area of the United States there were fewer than four thousand self-propelled vehicles of all kinds, and only about three hundred of these had petrol engines of anything like the type at which Henry Ford was now aiming.

He was quite sure in his own mind that he was doing the right thing. But there were many periods of anxiety, when he wondered if he was ever to make the grade, and prove himself as a car manufacturer.

Nevertheless, he soon started out. The Detroit Automobile Company was set up in 1899. The following year it was renamed the Ford Automobile Company. Henry convinced a group of businessmen in Detroit that, though this was in some respects a fairly speculative business, it was a business that had a considerable future. Henry, as has already been said, had very little money of his own, but these men put up the cash to enable him to start his own business. He was given a share in the company, in return for allowing them the use of his plans and models. He himself was paid a hundred dollars a month as chief engineer—less than he had been getting in his former job with the Edison Illuminating Company.

Henry had his own business now, in a sense; but he was to a large degree under the control of the men who had put up the capital. His ideas did not wholly chime with theirs. He wanted to make cheap cars in large numbers, to sell in a mass market which other manufacturers had never tapped to any degree. His financial supporters were not thinking on these lines at all. They were envisaging the production of a small number of cars at a high price, each car specially built for an assured buyer. Only thus, they felt, could the business be made to pay. And, since these men had put up the money to enable Henry to start his company, he had more or less to follow their instructions, though it irked him to have to do it.

The Henry Ford Company, therefore, during the first

year or two of its existence, concentrated on building a comparatively small number of good cars. Odd though it may seem, the original hand-built Ford cars were not unlike those being built by luxury companies which were usually regarded as being "prestige" firms, whereas Fords later won quite a different reputation: that of building plain, reliable cars at low prices. So, in 1902, Henry left the original share-holders, taking with him only his models and his drawings. No more luxury cars for him.

Henry now had some money behind him—for the twenty or thirty cars that he had built in the last couple of years had been sold at a pretty considerable profit. Since he had this cash available, Henry came to a new decision. Again it was something of a gamble. He had enough money, he thought, to live on for a year or so. Why not live on his capital and work on his ideas for new-style cars? Why not see if it would be possible to design a car which would sell at a price hitherto thought impossible? He could at the same time do something to explore the potential markets.

Few people at that time knew anything at all of how their cars ran; if a car broke down, they had to call in a skilled mechanic to get it going again. And Henry, from his past experience with farm machinery and with watches, knew that skilled mechanics were few and far between. A car breakdown, therefore, could be something of a tragedy to an owner.

Henry gave himself a year. Before the end of that time he was sure that he had a car which would sell. It was a reliable car, one which would not break down so often, and would not need to be repaired with such extreme care. If spare parts could be made readily available, any reasonably capable mechanic would be able to fit them. It was an altogether simpler affair than the earlier cars had been.

Yet now Henry Ford was faced with a new problem.

78

How was he to make his car known to prospective buyers? He had spent a good deal of his capital in modifying his original car so that it would be both cheaper and more reliable. He had little left for a massive advertising campaign. It would, he was convinced, need a lot of advertising to make his car known to the customers he knew were there. How to get hold of them?

By this time—in the early days of the twentieth century —a new sport was beginning to hit the headlines of the newspapers. This was motor-racing. Any car which won an important race was sure to get a lot of attention in the Press. This was free publicity; it would not need to be paid for, as ordinary advertising would. A big competition for racing cars would be big news.

Henry wondered if this was the answer. Could he build a car which would win races? Could his name reach the public by this means?

The champion racer at this time was a man called Alexander Winton, who came from Cleveland in Ohio. He had built a car which he called "The Bullet", and which had won almost every race in which it had been entered. Winton had challenged everyone to race against him. He was sure that his car was the fastest thing on four wheels, and that no one could possibly beat him in the normal racing conditions of the time.

Henry watched Winton in a race. He got as close a look at the Winton car as he could. He soon felt confident that he would be able to build a car which would have a good chance of beating "The Bullet" at its own game. For one thing, the Winton car, though it looked impressive, was, in Henry's opinion, far too heavy for the power of its engine. He was sure that if he built a lighter car, even though its engine might not be so powerful, it would beat Winton's massive machine.

Henry designed a new engine. He put it on a chassis that was not much more than a skeleton. The body was as light as he could possibly make it. Then he drove the car carefully to a straight stretch of country road outside Detroit, and gave it its head. Its speed astonished him, exceeding all his expectations.

Then he issued his challenge to Winton. The race was held at a track not far from Detroit. When Winton saw the flimsy-looking little Ford car he was almost openly contemptuous. But this did not worry Henry. He was very sure of himself by now.

Everyone who compared the two cars before the race began was sure that Winton would win. His car looked well-finished. Its bodywork shone in the winter sunshine. And on that December day in 1902 the Ford car looked poor and crude by comparison. But as the two cars started speeding around the track, there was no doubt which was the faster. Henry clung to the steering tiller like grim death, took the curves at what seemed an impossible speed, and emerged the winner, to the cheers of the crowd. He was now the racing champion of his country. And he had broken the speed record of his day, by covering a mile at about forty miles an hour—then something scarcely heard of.

At once offers came pouring in from all over the country. Many of those who had sneered now competed for the services of this unknown engineer who had built the wonder car. Business men with capital to invest offered to back Henry if he would start making his fast-moving car in greater numbers.

Henry was not yet prepared to start full-scale production, however. He had built the car in order to attract attention—and he had succeeded in doing that. But he knew that he could improve the design of his car, and probably improve its performance as well.

Those who had offered to back him did not for the most part understand what he was after. They did not know that he was keen to lower the price of cars, to reach a market which had not previously been considered. All through his career it was this that impelled Henry Ford. He wanted to make a car which everyone would be able to afford. He was not content to make cars which only the rich would be able to buy.

The car which had beaten "The Bullet" was a two-cylinder model. He now thought that a four-cylinder car might be even more successful, though the engine would be heavier. This would not merely beat the Winton car—it would beat any car in the world.

Henry now had a small staff helping him, the most note-worthy being a bicycle racer called Cooper whom Henry took into his confidence.

The two men set about designing a new car of a quite revolutionary type—a four-cylinder model which had the pulling power of eighty horses. An eighty-horse-power car had never been attempted at that time. The two men built two slightly different cars of this type. Cooper and Henry Ford, when they tried these cars out, were both terrified by the power they had created. They both said that they would have been scared to drive either car in a race.

Eventually they found a professional cyclist called Barney Oldfield who stated that he was prepared to drive anything, on two wheels or four. He had, in actual fact, never driven a motor-car of any kind. But he was prepared to have a go at this one.

Steering wheels had still not been introduced. The driver had to steer by means of a lever, called a tiller, rather like the lever used to steer a boat. Ford knew that to steer a car as powerful as his on a curving road, it would be necessary to have a powerful tiller, and one which could be easily controlled. So he designed a tiller which could be manipulated by using both hands. This two-handed tiller was only one of the revolutionary features of the new car, which was called the "999", after a famous express engine then in use on the railways.

Barney Oldfield was not scared, even when he went out on the track near Detroit where Henry had beaten Winton. The two-handed tiller was strong enough; and Oldfield had immensely powerful arms. But the track had many awkward bends, not easy to undertake.

Henry had designed the car with its weight low down, so that it would hug the road. He knew that it would be a difficult car to drive, but when Oldfield had spent some time driving it, both Henry and Tom Cooper were quite confident that their driver would break all the records there were.

The race was for three miles. Some six cars were entered, all of them driven by the top racing drivers of the time. People no longer sneered at the Ford car, even though the "999" still looked pretty crude in design. They remembered Henry's previous triumph and they were sure that his new model would prove as sensational as the old one had been. It moved with surprising ease. Barney Oldfield clung to the tiller with both hands, and let the car have its head. It soon built up to an incredible speed, even taking the difficult bends without slowing down.

More than once Henry, who was watching, held his breath, and wondered if Oldfield would be able to hold the car to the track. More than once it got perilously near the edge. But Oldfield was a genius of a driver, and he succeeded, somehow, in keeping the car moving at speed without quite reaching the tragic point of overturning it.

Oldfield had taken the lead right at the start. He never looked like losing that lead, and when he came to the end of the three-mile race he was a good half-mile ahead of his nearest rival.

Henry and Cooper solemnly shook hands. This was their moment of real triumph. They shook hands with Oldfield too, for it was his triumph no less than theirs. Oldfield was soon to become the most famous racing driver in America, if not in the world.

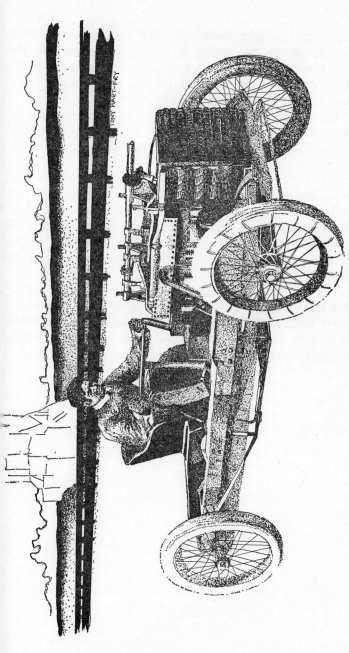

Barney Oldfield in the "999", Ford's record-breaking racing car which eventually covered a mile in under a minute

Oldfield, indeed, drove the "999" on several occasions in the months succeeding that first epic appearance. He improved on the speed record several times, and finally covered a mile in under a minute, which was a very surprising speed for the period.

Now Henry was satisfied. He had made his name so widely known that there should be no difficulty in getting himself to the top of the tree and achieving his great ambition.

The little Henry Ford Company could at once be wound up. Capital would, he thought, soon pour in. So the Ford Motor Company was registered. Twelve men subscribed its working capital. Henry himself had about a quarter of the shares, in return for which he contributed the design of his car, and gave the new company all rights in its manufacture.

Henry's one regret was that his father had not lived to see him established in the world of car-building. He would have liked to have had the chance to prove his father wrong in thinking that the only real future lay in unmechanized farming.

CHAPTER SEVEN

THE COMPANY ESTABLISHED

Henry Ford had always turned his face against a work-man's being a jack of all trades. One of the objections that he had had against some of the firms he had worked for had been that they had expected everyone to do every-thing. But now he was committed to doing almost every-thing for the Ford Motor Company. Officially he was chief engineer; actually he did most of the managerial work, and he also designed the cars. In addition he often had to take a turn at the bench, working a lathe or operating some other piece of machinery. He was sure, however, that this was only a temporary matter, and that, when the company became really well-established, he would be able to spend all his time as designer and chief engineer, leaving the more routine tasks to mechanics and other assistants in the works.

The "works" at present consisted of a small wooden shed. His staff consisted of two men. They were capable mech-anics, but that was all. There was a certain amount of equipment, but not much. It was not at present possible for Henry and his two assistants to make all the com-ponents from which he intended to build his Ford cars. All that, too, lay in the future.

Henry had worked out fairly detailed designs for the cars he wanted to build. These designs included engineering drawings of many of the component parts. His early idea was that the components should be made under contract by various firms in Detroit. One firm would make the bodies; another would make the wheels; others the cylinders, pistons and so on. When all the parts had been made under contract, Henry and his two mechanics would only have to fasten them together.

At first there was some difficulty in finding firms which would and could make the components. Detroit was something of an engineering city; but some of the things which Henry wanted made were so different from those other motor manufacturers wanted that even firms specializing in making car parts found it difficult to provide just what Henry had ordered. There were "teething troubles" as well, for sometimes parts that were supposed to fasten together did not quite fit, and then the designs had to be checked and the contracting engineers given new instructions.

Henry had some success in selling cars right from the start. The first type he made was called the Model A. This was a two-seater, though a body seating four people instead of two could be fitted at extra cost. Lamps, horn, and windscreen were also fitted at charges which were additional to the basic price of the car. The petrol tank would hold five gallons of petrol (about 22 litres), and the engine was an eight-horse-power one.

The first car was finished in June, and was sold in July. Before the company had been in operation for a year, well over a thousand cars had been sold. Henry was delighted. This was what he had been aiming at for years, and now he saw all his confidence in himself justified, though he was being paid only two hundred dollars a month, and there was sometimes a certain amount of difficulty in drawing his pay. When a car was sold, the money had to be used to pay the component manufacturers for new bodies or engines or wheels for the next batch of cars to be assembled. So there was not much fluid cash, even to pay those who were working in the little factory.

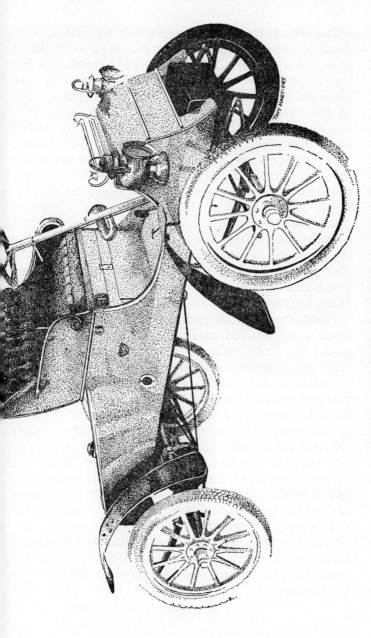

A Model A Ford: the first of this type was built in 1903

In a very short time, Henry was able to tell Clara that the Ford car was already acquiring a reputation for being reliable. Quite early on, too, he worked to persuade a few agents spread all over the country to keep a stock of Ford spare parts. In those days that was very important; some of the foreign cars imported into America were quite reliable as long as they were running, but if some part of the engine cracked, or some mechanical fault showed itself, it might mean a wait of weeks or even months while the spare part was shipped over from Europe. Sometimes, even, the part was impossible to get, and a replacement had to be made by hand. This was again liable to be a long and a costly business.

Henry knew all this. He had heard people grumbling at the long delay in getting a replacement for a broken part. He was eager, as soon as his cars began to sell in considerable numbers, to prove that good servicing was to be part of his regular policy.

Another point which made Ford cars popular was that, when once a car had been proved satisfactory, the same model was to be made for several years on end. Some firms had already started making revolutionary changes in their cars each year. Henry was concerned to keep his customers, and so he was keen to design a car that would last. That meant a car which would not change much from year to year, so that a set of spare parts made one year would still fit a car made a year or two later.

Some of those who had helped Henry Ford by putting up the money which enabled him to start his business did not altogether agree with him. They thought that, since a car had always been a kind of luxury article used by the rich, it would be a more sensible procedure to show the rich customers a new and more modern-looking model each year. Henry disagreed, but he could not argue too much with the people who had provided him with his working capital.

So in 1904 there were three models. There was a Model B, a four-cylinder affair. There was a two-cylinder car, an improved Model A, now to be called Model C. There was a somewhat more elaborate car, called Model F. What happened to Model D and Model E is not recorded. Perhaps they were unsuccessful experimental cars which, with his usual acumen, Henry discarded.

Model B, at all events, was the first four-cylinder Ford. In a new effort to get publicity for this, Henry announced that he would drive a Model B car against time on the frozen surface of Lake St. Claire, not far from Detroit. Clara was very worried at this. She had visions of her husband going through the ice and being drowned. Henry himself was not altogether happy about it, the more so in that there were a number of small cracks in the ice, and he wondered what would happen when he drove a car across the surface at high speed. But the run had been announced; the papers had made a lot of fuss about it. Henry knew that if he now cancelled or postponed the run, he would be in for trouble.

He was in enough trouble as it was. The cracks in the ice made steering very difficult. The car bounced and skidded. But there was no tragedy. The ice did not break. And Henry was timed over a measured mile, which he covered in just under fifty seconds—a very remarkable speed for the period. Indeed, it cut several seconds off what was then the world speed record. So it was a good event from the point of view of publicity.

However, the price of cars had gone up. Henry's financial backers more or less forced him to put up prices, against his better judgment. The result was that fewer cars were sold than in the previous year, though the figure reached one thousand five hundred—better than at the very beginning.

Henry now had a fair amount of money of his own. He decided that there was only one thing to be done. He had many a discussion about this with Clara. She understood his desire to keep prices down. But she felt that he was taking a considerable risk if he cut prices too much.

"There's only one way out of all this, Clara," he said one night when they were sitting beside the fire.

"And what is that?" she asked quietly.

"I must hold a majority holding in the company."

"What do you mean?"

Henry grinned that lean grin of his. "If I own more than half the shares in the company, they can't dictate to me about policy. Whatever I want to do with the company will be done."

"But how can you get more than half the shares in the company?" his wife asked.

"Buy them!" he snapped.

And he did just that. In 1906 he used all his savings to buy shares in the company. In a few months nearly sixty per cent of the shares were his own personal property, and he was beyond the control of his business partners. Now he could do just what he wanted. He could raise or lower prices as he wished. He could make one model or ten. No one could argue with him or deny him. He was in a sense the dictator of the Ford Motor Company's affairs. That those affairs flourished so well was a tribute to Henry Ford's great business ability.

He now made only one type of engine, though the style of the car body could be varied. He brought the cheapest model down to six hundred dollars in price, which was within range of most working men. That year he sold over eight thousand cars—five times as many as in any previous year. There could be no doubt at all that Henry's new policy was paying off.

Henry had all the affairs of the company in his own hands, and he was beginning to wonder if it was not time to begin making some of the component parts himself, instead of buying them from other firms and then assembling the cars in the Ford shops. Assembly was a fairly quick process; on one day in 1906 a hundred cars were assembled.

It was time to get bigger premises. In 1906 a big new three-storey building was erected. Here Ford made a start on the manufacture of some of the components.

The process of appointing Ford agents to cover the country now increased. Most cars had previously been sold direct from the factory, but Henry knew that he would not be able to get people to stock and sell spare parts unless they were also able to sell Ford cars, with a suitable discount so that they would make a small profit on each deal.

He insisted, however, that the agent must not just provide a sales point where cars and spares could be bought; he would also have to employ capable mechanics so that any owner of a Ford car would be able to rely on getting any necessary repairs done without undue delay.

Henry's efforts to give the customers a satisfactory deal, together with the cheapness of the cars that he was making, did not make him exactly a popular man in the motor trade. Moreover, his very success made him a suitable target for Mr. George Selden, that lawyer who had registered a rather vague but very comprehensive patent some years before.

In 1903 a group of manufacturers had agreed with Mr. Selden that they would recognize his patent. They had also agreed that no other firms would be allowed to join their group in future. This should have meant that no new car manufacturer would be able to break into the market— which was just what Henry was doing, and doing with very great success, selling more cars than anyone else in the business.

The association of manufacturers paid a royalty to Mr. Selden on every car they made. Henry, after studying all the facts, decided that he was making a car very different from those being made by the group. He therefore refused to pay the royalty. It was a very bold decision, and it caused Clara to worry. She had visions of Henry having to go through the courts and pay huge amounts in damages. Henry did not care. He was very conscious of being in the right.

The lawsuit which developed went on for years. Much of what we know of the early days of the Ford Motor Company comes from the evidence which Henry gave in court. In 1909 a district court upheld the patent. Henry, however, went on turning out cars by the thousand. The struggle went on.

The group who had accepted the Selden patent had published advertisements warning car buyers not to spend money on Ford cars, which were, they said, infringing patent rights.

Henry hit back with a big advertisement in the principal papers all over the country. In this he said that every buyer of a Ford car would be given a bond, protecting him against any claim from the patent-holders. It ended: "The bond is yours for the asking, so do not allow yourself to be sold inferior cars at extravagant prices because of any statement made by this 'Divine' body."

The Selden attempt to impress the American public failed. Henry had retained the confidence of the car buyers. In 1909, for instance, some eighteen thousand Ford cars were sold, and under a hundred of the buyers asked for the bond.

Henry was now becoming known to the American public as something of a "character". He gave the public value for money in the cars which he sold them—but he often gave them a chuckle as well. He was down-to-earth. "If a car which I made breaks down," he said, "I know that I am to blame." The Ford made in those early days was simpler than most cars of the period. "Anyone," Henry said, "can drive a Ford." Ford jokes, which went the rounds for many years, were already beginning to cir-

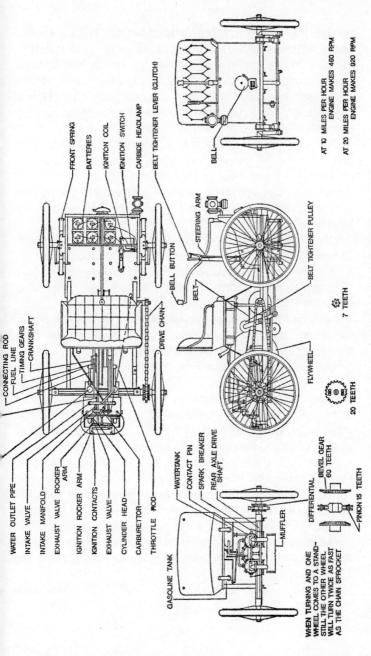

WATER OUTLET PIPE
INTAKE VALVE
INTAKE MANIFOLD
EXHAUST VALVE ROCKER ARM
IGNITION ROCKER ARM
IGNITION CONTACTS
EXHAUST VALVE
CYLINDER HEAD
CARBURETTOR
THROTTLE ROD

CONNECTING ROD
FUEL LINE
TIMING GEARS
CRANKSHAFT

FRONT SPRING
BATTERIES
IGNITION COIL
IGNITION SWITCH
CARBIDE HEADLAMP
BELT TIGHTENER LEVER (CLUTCH)

BELL BUTTON
DRIVE CHAIN

STEERING ARM
BELL

BELT
BELT TIGHTENER PULLEY

FLYWHEEL
7 TEETH
20 TEETH

GASOLINE TANK
WATERTANK
CONTACT PIN
SPARK BREAKER
REAR AXLE DRIVE SHAFT
MUFFLER

DIFFERENTIAL
BEVEL GEAR 60 TEETH
PINION 15 TEETH

WHEN TURNING AND ONE
WHEEL COMES TO A STAND—
STILL THE OTHER WHEEL
WILL TURN TWICE AS FAST
AS THE CHAIN SPROCKET

AT 10 MILES PER HOUR
ENGINE MAKES 460 RPM

AT 20 MILES PER HOUR
ENGINE MAKES 920 RPM

Working drawings of an early Ford production model

culate—jokes which often rebounded to Ford's credit. There were cartoons, for instance, showing men standing ruefully by an expensive-looking car which had broken down: a rather scruffy-looking Ford, meanwhile, drove cheerfully by. This was the sort of joke that Henry appreciated, for it underlined his own desire to create an impression of dependability.

And some of his answers to counsel during the lawsuit about the Selden patent made good reading. People began to think of Henry Ford as the real self-made American.

For example, counsel asked: "Do you think the Selden patent has been of any benefit in your business of making automobiles in the past?"

"Yes," said Henry and paused. Counsel was surprised, as Henry had been all the time arguing that his cars in no way infringed the Selden patent. Then Henry added: "There has been helpful publicity for us, which we have obtained through fighting the patent."

The great American public chuckled at the way in which the blunt, outspoken man from Detroit could outwit even the clever lawyers who were trying to tie him into knots.

The lawsuit went on and on. Finally, in 1911, there were further efforts to enforce the Selden patent. But the court decided that the patent was (in legal terms) "valid but not infringed". This was something of a triumph for Henry, who had always argued that his cars, whatever their model, did not owe anything to any previous experimenter. His aim had always been to make a car which would be easy to drive and which would have several years of life, so that it would not need replacing in a very short time. He also aimed, right from the start, at producing a vehicle which could be kept in good running order, with spare parts in easy supply. Agents selling cars and spares were now being appointed in considerable numbers all over the United States.

The story soon went the rounds that Ford cars were

reliable. There was one Model A Ford, which was bought by a man in California in 1904. It went on running, under various owners, for three years or so, and in 1907 it was sold to a man who lived in mountainous country where the roads were often little more than tracks. This owner drove it for no less than eight years, and in 1915, when the car was eleven years old, a later owner took out the engine and used it to run a water-pump on his farm. Eleven years running on poor roads is a longer history than most cars were able to boast.

One thing which contributed to the success of the early cars was Henry's deep understanding of the ways in which metals of various kinds could be used. Often, when a car had run for some thousands of miles, he would strip the engine down and examine and test each component part carefully to see how it was standing up to wear. If he found, for example, that one bearing was wearing more than others, he might decide that some slight adjustment was needed, or that a harder or better kind of steel would have to be used at that point.

This was one of the very real advantages of having a man at the head of affairs who knew the bases of engine-building. Henry's petrol-driven engines looked very different from the steam-engines on which he had worked for so many years, but the mechanical principles were not all that different, and he was able to tell just what was going wrong and just what was needed to put it right.

As soon as he had got complete control of the company, Henry started work on improving the design of his engines. He still had at the back of his mind the idea that most car manufacturers made a mistake in spreading their interests over many different models, of different design and different horse-power. Only by building one model and sticking to it, he thought, would it be possible to get the utmost efficiency out of his plant. He wanted to make all the component parts himself, and if he were concentrating on one model, and one only, this would be far easier—it would be much more difficult to build parts for half-a-dozen different sorts of engine.

In the period of 1908–1909, there were still a number of different Ford models being made. Over ten thousand cars were sold, and Henry was not dissatisfied. He was now making a lot of money, even though he was keeping prices low. Since he owned more than half the shares in the company, more than half the total profits came into his pocket. He was still at that time defying the law courts over the matter of the Selden patent, but he was not worried—he was sure that in the end the case would be decided in his favour. And he was also sure that he would finally achieve his ambition by concentrating on one extremely popular model, thus turning out thousands of cars for which there would be a ready-made demand.

In 1909 there was launched what came to be called the Model T—it was, in the end, to be the most famous car ever made in the world. This was the prototype of what jokers called the "Tin Lizzie". The car gave rise to many sneers and many comic drawings. But it outsold all its rivals, and proved to be the final builder of the Ford fortunes.

The Model T was in that first year competing with two others—Model R and Model S—but these were by no means as successful. (Some letters of the Ford alphabet were missing, because some experimental models proved not to be as good as originally hoped; Henry never had the slightest hesitation in scrapping a car which did not come up to his expectations.) The Model T, however, far exceeded those expectations. It sold better than any other model which the Ford factory had hitherto made. Henry was sure that he was on a winner.

"That's the best selling car of the lot," he told Clara, when he came home one day, after a detailed study of the order books. Henry was not just a mechanic and an engineer; he was also, though self-taught, something of an accountant, and he was quite capable of working out just what was paying and what was losing money.

"You're happy about it, Henry?" she asked. Now that little Edsel was growing up, she was able to take an interest in the business again, more than when all her attention had been concentrated on the baby.

"I'm sure happy!" Henry exclaimed, his eyes sparkling with enthusiasm. "It will sell in millions before we've finished with it."

"Millions?" She did not really believe this. She thought that it was just part of Henry's over-optimistic way of looking at things.

"Yes," he said. "Millions."

Clara Ford tried to imagine millions of cars driving over the rough and unsatisfactory roads which still existed in many parts of America. She found the effort beyond her.

"I'm going to concentrate on the Model T, Clara," Henry said. "This is a winner, and when you find a good thing in business, you put all your money in it."

Clara was a bit doubtful. "Isn't that a little bit like what my mother used to call putting all your eggs in one basket?" she objected.

Henry snorted. "Why not—if it's a good basket?" he asked.

Now, day by day, he examined the sales book and the order book. There was only one question in his mind. How was the Model T going? Was it keeping up its success? Was it still far outstripping the other models which were still in production? He talked it over with some of the salesmen he employed, visiting agents and garages from New York to California. Few of the salesmen had any doubt that the Model T Ford was a roaring success; but few of them would agree with Henry when he said that he was thinking of dropping some of the less popular models, and concentrating on the most popular one.

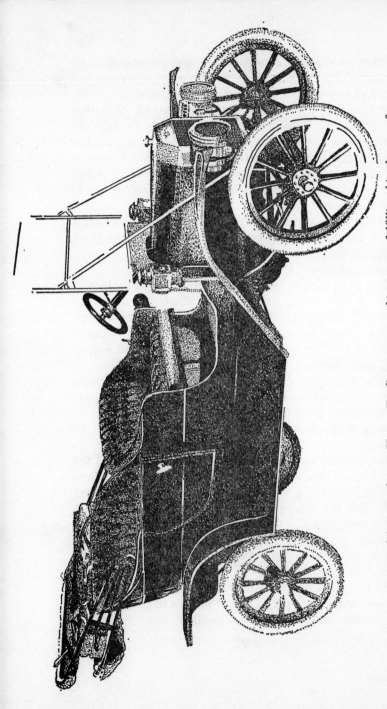

The Model T Ford was Henry Ford's greatest achievement, fulfilling his dream of producing a car which would be cheap enough and reliable enough to put it in reach of the ordinary working man. The first Model T was made in 1909, the last in 1927; for seven-

"Some people want a bit better car, Mr. Ford," said one of his sales staff, when Henry was praising the Model T.

"How many people?" Henry asked.

The salesman grinned. "Oh, yes, I know," he said. "If you get out a very cheap car, and it's still reliable, hundreds of people will buy it. Something a bit more classy at a higher price won't sell in as great numbers. But the guy who is prepared to pay a few hundred dollars more is still a customer."

"But is the guy who will spend a few hundred dollars more the sort of customer that we want?" Henry asked.

"That's your affair, Mr. Ford," said the salesman. "My job is to sell the cars that you make. It's for you to decide what those cars will be. But I still think that a classier car at a higher price is worth making, even if you don't sell as many of them."

Henry had many conversations of this kind. He was not yet quite committed to putting all his eggs in one basket, but he was moving in that direction. Would it be possible, he asked himself, to persuade both his sales staff and his customers that if Fords concentrated on making one model and one only, they could improve the service that they were offering the public?

Henry Ford had several times taken what his business friends called a gamble. He knew that if he came to this decision, they would think it the greatest gamble of his whole career. Could he take the risk? For some time he hovered on the brink.

CHAPTER EIGHT

THE BEST-SELLER

One of the best-kept secrets in the history of the automobile industry was Henry Ford's final decision in this matter of concentrating on the Model T car.

No earlier announcements had been made. Orders for other models had been accepted up to the night before. Then one morning in 1910 an announcement hit the headlines of all the newspapers. This announcement was to the effect that from now on Fords would be making one model only—the Model T. The chassis on which the body was mounted would be the same for every car. The engine would be identical. Spare parts would be kept by every Ford agent throughout the United States, and would be readily available to any motorist who wanted to repair his car.

One of Henry's most-quoted jokes dates from this announcement. He had been describing the reasons for his decision. Then he added: "Any customer can have his car painted any colour that he wants so long as it's black."

This was a bombshell for the motor industry. It was even a bombshell for Ford salesmen, most of whom thought that it would be hopeless to try to sell to the motoring public if there were only one Ford car available. All manufacturers making cars at this time were able to offer their customers a variety of models at a variety of prices; and if Ford could provide one car only, a customer who did not want that particular model would be compelled to go to another manufacturer.

"O.K. Let him go to another manufacturer," Henry said, when this point was made one day at a conference at the works. "We'll get the big market, and we shan't need to bother about the rich man who wants a more showy car. There are a lot more people who can afford our prices than there are people who can afford the higher prices other guys are charging. If they don't like our product, let them get another. Who cares? I don't, anyway."

Henry Ford might not care. But his salesmen did. They made their living by selling cars, and they feared that if they had only one model to sell, this might result in a big drop in their income.

"There will be a big saving in cost," Henry pointed out at this conference.

"Maybe that's so, Mr. Ford," said one of his best salesmen. "But what do we say to the man who wants what they are now calling a quality car?"

"Tell him that ours is a quality car, but at a lower price than anyone else can quote," Henry said.

The salesman looked very doubtful at this argument. He thought that he knew his customers, and that he would not be able to convince the wealthier ones that it would be worth their while buying a car which looked just the same —which *was*, indeed, just the same—as the car someone with a lot less money would be able to buy.

"Each year, if sales build up, we shall be able to lower the price," Henry pointed out.

"You think so, Mr. Ford?" This was the same star salesman who had spoken before.

"I'm certain."

Henry took advertising space in the papers to announce his decision. The advertisement stated that the Ford car "will be so low in price that no man making a good salary will be unable to own one—and enjoy with his family the blessing of hours of pleasure in God's great open spaces."

Makers of more expensive cars laughed at that advertisement. They were sure that this effort could not succeed. They were sure that Henry Ford was crazy to attempt to cheapen cars to the extent he hoped. They were sure that it would bring him to bankruptcy.

All those who made bigger and more expensive cars were certain that the motor-car was a luxury article, to be bought by business men and important people who wanted to show off, acting as if they had even more money than they did. An ordinary car which looked what it was—a utility article which might be reliable but was not in any way luxurious—would never have any sort of appeal for rich people. Ford's rivals thought that rich people were the only ones who would buy cars—and they would not wish to be seen driving cars which were identical with those being driven by poorer folk.

Many of the shareholders, too, were doubtful at this new policy. They felt that Henry was taking a great risk with the money that they had put into the company. But since Henry owned more than half the shares, there was little they could do about it. He was able to make his own decisions, and to stick by them, no matter what his critics might say.

He took another too. He was sure that his new policy would be a great success. If it proved as successful as he expected, he would need a far bigger factory. So he boldly went out and bought up sixty acres (twenty-four hectares) of land at a place called Highland Park, some miles out of Detroit. Here a vast new factory soon began to take shape. This Henry did not build on borrowed money, as many people would have done. He did not believe in running his business on money borrowed from a bank, which would charge him a high rate of interest. He wanted to finance his undertakings out of the year-by-year profits of the company. He therefore raised the price of the Model T, so that the profit would enable him to build the factory without raising a bank loan. This, too, aroused criticism,

102

both from his salesmen and from the shareholders in the company.

By the end of 1910, however, it was clear that the new policy had paid off. Nearly nineteen thousand cars were sold in a period of twelve months. The new factory was now available. It was far more convenient than the old cramped premises had been. There was much less need for the workers to waste time carrying tools or components about, for these were arranged, as far as possible, within easy reach of the appropriate work-benches. The result was that by 1911 Henry found that a first reduction in cost could be put into effect, as he had forecast. That year over thirty-four thousand Ford cars were sold. Now the critics were silent. Henry Ford alone had felt confidence in his policy. All the experts, whether salesmen or rivals, had thought that he was wrong. But he had proved himself right. He felt more and more happy as the months went by.

The first factory covered less than three acres (1·2 hectares), though Henry had taken the precaution of buying far more land than would at first be necessary. In a year or two massive extensions were added to the new factory; soon it occupied over thirty acres (twelve hectares), and the number of men working there nearly doubled.

It was at this time, too, that Henry came to see that there was a market for the Model T in Europe as well as in the United States. The popularity of the Ford car in Great Britain had first emerged in 1905 when a Ford car had taken part in a reliability trial over some hundreds of miles in the Scottish mountains. In 1911 a Model T was driven up Ben Nevis. This mountain, nearly 5000 feet (1500 metres) high, had never before been scaled in a car. Sales in Britain began to rise, and in that same year over fourteen thousand Fords were sold on the European side of the Atlantic. At first the cars were shipped across the Atlantic ready-built; later, parts were exported to Britain,

103

and a factory was opened in Manchester where American-made components were assembled.

Henry had in the beginning rarely thought of himself as anything like an international figure. He had designed his cars simply for the American market. But it now began to become obvious that a car which sold so well in the American market appealed to foreign markets as well.

The success of the Model T Ford was probably the most sensational that the motor industry has ever seen. Henry Ford, whose early efforts had been so sneered at by his business rivals, had proved himself beyond all doubt.

He was still by no means convinced that he had found the cheapest methods of production. Within a few years of Ford's beginning to make his own components, most of the parts from which his cars were assembled were made by the four thousand workers in the big new factory at Highland Park. But Henry was not satisfied. When he wandered around the factory, he still saw men carrying things from one workshop to another. He always felt that this was one of the greatest possible wastes of time and effort. "Pedestrianism," he said once in those early days, "is not a very well-paid line." Some of the parts, which were made in the small workshops, had to be carried considerable distances to the assembly point. Was there any way to get over it?

There was also the point—never far from Henry's mind—that many of his workers were not as specialized as he would have liked. Many of the men were still required to do many different jobs. This, too, he felt to be a grave mistake. If a man was given one job to do, and left to it, he would get better and better at it as time went on.

The two problems—the need to fetch and carry within the factory, and the lack of specialized skills—were really, Henry came to think, two parts of one problem. How was he to overcome them?

During those years from 1910 to 1913, while the sales of

104

Ford cars went steadily up and the price went steadily down, Henry spent much time thinking about this.

Edsel was by now working with his father. Henry, who had not received much formal education himself, did not propose to send the boy to college. One day, when he himself retired, his son would take over the Ford Company. Henry therefore introduced him into the various fields of the factory's production, and decided that he would give the boy a general knowledge, practical as well as theoretical, of the way in which the Ford car was manufactured.

"Too much walking about," Henry said to Edsel one day. "That's the great trouble. They nearly fall over each other sometimes, carrying tools or parts from one place to another."

"But all factories work like that," Edsel objected.

"All other factories may do that," Henry agreed. "But that is no reason why *my* factory should do that. There must be a more efficient way of working the thing. And all this bending and stooping—that's bad too. The men's backs ache. They get tired sooner. And a tired worker is not an efficient worker."

"Well, what do you think we can do?" Edsel asked. He did not see just what his father was proposing.

"Specialize. Give each man one job, and let him do that job over and over."

"It'll be dull, doing one thing over and over," Edsel objected.

"No matter; a man won't mind doing a dull job if he's well paid," Henry said. "If we can work it out so as to cut costs, we shall be able to pay higher wages. Then we'll see that the whole thing will work out. If we go on as we're doing now, there is a limit to how much we can cut costs and reduce prices. There ought to be no limit."

It was not until 1913 that Henry first began to put into effect this new idea which in later years was to be called "time and motion study"—that is, a way of reducing the need for a factory worker to move about, either in the course of actually doing his job, or in fetching the tools or the materials needed for that job.

Ford had spent a lot of time in thinking out the new methods of production which he had already discussed with Edsel. He had not at first found his son very responsive, though he was quite sure in his own mind that Edsel would fit in with any scheme which might be brought forward.

The idea which Henry worked out was eventually to be called an assembly line. This was a moving conveyor belt which trundled along past one worker after another. Each man could carry out his own small task in the assembling of a component, so that as it was carried along the belt, from worker to worker, it grew closer and closer to completion, stage by stage, until at last it was finished.

To begin with, he did not see how this idea could be applied to the assembly of a complete motor car, or even a complete engine for a motor car, but he thought that it might perhaps be possible to use such an assembly method on some small but moderately complicated part of the engine, such as the magneto. This, he was sure, would cut down the time that it would take to put a magneto together. Time was money. If a magneto could be assembled in half the time, the cost of producing it would be correspondingly reduced.

Up to this time several men had worked to assemble a magneto from its component parts. It had been necessary for each man to handle more than twenty pieces. Henry Ford's first experiment in conveyor belt assembly was this operation. He split up the assembly work into more than twenty separate stages, each one simple and each one designed to be carried out by a different man as the small conveyor belt moved slowly past. This cut the time of making the magneto by more than half. Henry was satisfied that he had been right; this was one of the ways in which costs could be cut. He also saw that his original conveyor belt was a little too low for the men to work at it comfortably, and he therefore had it raised a little way. This almost halved the time again. Finally, he realized that the men were working well within their capacity, so that it might be possible to have the conveyor belt speeded up somewhat. This was tried out, and in the end the most satisfactory speed was found. The belt had to move fast enough to produce good results, but not so fast that the pieces of assembly work done by each man were violently rushed. Eventually Henry found that the whole job of assembling the magneto could be done in about a quarter of the time that had been needed under the original system.

There were those who said that Henry Ford was a slave-driver, that men were becoming slaves to a machine. But the fact remained that they were well-paid for their work. Edsel had thought it would be dull work; undeniably it was sometimes dull. But at the same time Henry's feeling was justified: the men did not mind so much doing dull, routine tasks, if they were well-paid for doing them.

Gradually this assembly-line method was extended. Soon the whole engine was being put together by this method. Formerly over eighty operations had been needed to build an engine, and each man had done the work painfully slowly. If Henry was to maintain his promise of reducing the price of the product from year to year, he knew that he would have to lower the cost of production. The best way of doing this was undoubtedly mass-production by means of a conveyor-belt system.

Ford was the first large-scale manufacturer in the world to introduce this mass-production system. More than eighty men were now engaged on the assembly-line. The time it took to assemble an engine was greatly reduced. And the old method of individual assembly was abandoned.

A magneto is assembled by the conveyor belt method, which Ford put into effect in 1913; the new assembly method cut down costs by reducing the amount of time spent on assembly. Ford was the first large-scale manufacturer in the world to introduce this mass-production system

But what about the chassis? The framework on which the engine and the body were eventually mounted was a far bigger and clumsier thing than the engine itself. Would it be possible to assemble a chassis by a conveyor-belt, assembly-line method? The sheer size and difficulty of handling a car's chassis would have put off any lesser man.

But Henry Ford was not put off. His new method of assembly had proved itself with smaller things, like engines. And engines, though smaller, were much more complex than the chassis. Surely, he told himself, it should be possible to work out a scheme so that a chassis could be put together more satisfactorily than by the old method.

Clearly the size made a different method of working necessary, even though the general principle might be the same. Why not, he asked himself one day, have the chassis on the end of a rope, controlled by a windlass and trolley?

This idea came one night. The next morning Henry walked around the factory, seeing if he could find a suitable spot to try it out. He needed plenty of room, for the rope would have to be a long one. The men working on the assembly would probably not be able to stand still and let the slowly-growing chassis move past them. They would have to walk alongside it. The component parts could be stored on benches on either side. The men could walk alongside the moving chassis, pick up the parts which it was their job to fit, and fasten them into position—And in the end a completed chassis would be released at the other end of the large workshop.

Henry already had a group of men who were fairly happy about working on an assembly-line. Now he called a meeting of these men and told them what he was proposing to do. Henry was never a great believer in democracy on the workshop floor, but when he had a new and revolutionary idea to put into operation, he believed in taking into his confidence the men who would, after all, be needed to get that operation moving properly.

The men, while quite prepared to try the thing out, were by no means convinced that this would be a workable scheme. Henry himself was quite sure. And when the chosen half-dozen men had been given time to get accustomed to the new method, it was found that the time it took them to assemble a chassis had been cut to less than half what it had been under the old system. Later on, when the number of parts handled by each man was reduced, the time was cut even further. More men were, of course, employed; they were highly paid, too. But the increased production was such as to reduce the cost per chassis fairly considerably.

It has already been said that Henry thought most factory work involved too much stooping and bending. When he introduced a new method of this kind, he was always keen to get the conveyor belt at the height which would be most comfortable for those working at it. But in such a matter as the chassis-assembly, this was not easy. The men had to pick up various parts and insert them at various points. These points were at sundry different heights; and the men, too, were of sundry different heights. A conveyor belt which was at a convenient height for a very tall man might not be anything like as suitable for a man who was only of moderate height.

So Henry spent a considerable time in experimenting. He had conveyor belts fitted at various heights from the floor, and got a group of men of different heights to work at them for several hours each. Then he asked the men to report if they found the height convenient or tiring. Soon he was able to arrive at two heights which seemed most generally suitable. The chassis was now assembled at about waist-level—that is, the waist-level of an average man. Extremely tall men or extremely short men were not given tasks on this assembly. But the two heights which Henry eventually settled on appeared to suit the majority of his workers.

Henry now had to study his workmen, so that they could be enabled to work in comfort but, at the same time, fast enough and well enough to increase production as much as was humanly possible. The problem of deciding on the speed of the conveyor-belt, which had shown itself when this method of assembly was first tried out, now arose again. He found the best way was to start the belt moving at a very slow speed, so that each man got his work done long before the line moved on. Then, bit by bit, the speed would be increased, until a speed was found which was clearly too great, for the chassis work moved on before each man could complete his task. Thus, for any particular operation, Henry and his engineers knew which speed was too slow and which speed was too fast. A little more experimentation enabled them to find the speed in between these two extremes which could be expected to give the best possible results.

In the years between 1911 and 1913 the assembly-line method rapidly increased its scope. Henry was now putting into operation what he had said to his father on the farm, years before. He was cutting down the hard slog of hand labour, and using machines to carry out swiftly tasks which men took much longer to do.

The Ford factory soon looked different from any other factory of its day. The average factory at that time had a host of workers scurrying about, taking tools or raw materials from one spot to another. In the Ford factory the men for the most part stood still, and the conveyor belt brought the tools and raw materials to the workers. There were some machines, such as those stamping small pieces of metal like washers or discs out of sheet metal, which Henry thought could run perfectly well without a man in charge, save to replace the sheet metal as it became exhausted. So these machines were made completely automatic. No one watched them. An alarm bell would ring if the machine went wrong. Otherwise, it went on chugging away, producing its components, apparently without any human assistance. Any man who had been working such a machine was switched to do another job. No man was dismissed; no man "got the sack". The demand for Ford cars was building up so fast that a man whose job vanished could always depend on a new job

111

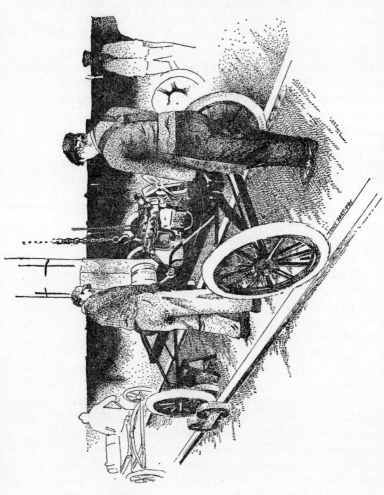

Following the success of the conveyor-belt assembly method with the magneto, Ford adapted it for other production operations. Illustrated here is the use of the

offering itself—and usually a new job at a higher rate of pay than the old one.

Henry had always believed in giving an honest day's wage for an honest day's work. His workmen had helped him to make a fortune. He knew that, without hard work by a good many people, he would never have made Ford cars the success that they were.

By 1914 about half a million people were riding in Ford cars, but few of them knew very much about the man who designed those cars and who was even yet supervising their production in that factory outside Detroit. Henry had never sought anything in the way of personal publicity for himself. When he had won those sensational races he had not done so to make himself famous, but to make it possible for him to build and sell more cars than before.

Then, in 1914, Henry announced that all Ford workers would be given a minimum wage of five dollars a day, and that the working hours in the factory would be shortened from nine to eight. The general wage for similar jobs elsewhere in the United States was less than three dollars a day; the average working day was nine hours. The papers said that this meant that Ford was giving away something like ten million dollars in a year—about half the profit that the Ford Company was expecting to make in 1914.

Shareholders were not keen, though they were powerless to stop it as Henry held a majority of the shares. But the new idea meant that Henry now had the absolute pick of the skilled mechanics. On the day after this announcement, there was a milling crowd of thousands of men at the gates of the factory, eagerly seeking the opportunity to work there. The police had to be called in, but so vast was the crowd of would-be workers that even the police could not control them. Henry did not worry. He was, he knew, doing his best for himself, his company and his workmen. The excited crowds would be a nine-day-wonder. It would die away. But meanwhile the publicity, after all, did not do the Ford Motor Company any harm.

CHAPTER NINE

GREAT MAN ACKNOWLEDGED

Many of those critics who had accused Henry of being crazy when he had taken his earlier decisions about his methods of work, the price of selling his cars, and the types of car which he proposed to make, now renewed that sort of criticism. Some of the newspapers said that this unheard-of step—giving away millions of dollars to his workmen—was something that would never succeed. Others called Henry an "inspired millionaire". At a flower show in New York a new orchid was named "Mr. and Mrs. Henry Ford". Someone said that to have a flower called after you is the highest kind of compliment that anyone can receive. The popular magazines published stories of the Ford family, with a series of illustrations showing the methods of mass-production in the factory.

It was some time before the sensation of the increased wage and the great hand-out of cash began to die down. Henry was fairly besieged by newspaper reporters. He left Detroit and tried to get a little peace and quiet away from home. But when he reached New York he found a queue of reporters and Press photographers waiting for him. After three days dodging these men as best he could, he went back to Detroit again. But once more the men from the newspapers haunted him. He could not refuse to meet them, since, like every big businessman, he was to some extent dependent on Press publicity in making his cars known to the public. The goodwill of the Press was part of the stock-in-trade of his business, and he knew that

115

it was no use upsetting the papers. After all, he told Clara, these men, who seemed to find his actions so exciting and so important, were giving Ford cars many millions of dollars' worth of free publicity in all that they were writing and publishing about the leader of the Ford empire.

So he suddenly found himself rocketed into the papers. No reporter worth his salt would turn down an opportunity to talk to Henry Ford. He was interviewed, and his opinions were asked, on every subject under the sun. Quite suddenly he found himself accepted and acknowledged as a great man, whose ideas about anything and everything were eagerly canvassed.

The American Press in those days thought that every eminent man should be listened to on every subject, including those about which he knew very little. So it was that Henry Ford was reported as saying a whole host of things on a whole host of subjects. Some of the things he said were wise; some of them were foolish. The foolish sayings generally came when he ventured outside the world of business, and especially engineering, in which he was most at home.

He praised hard-working men. He said: "Work is the greatest blessing", which amused some people and annoyed others. He did not drink and did not smoke, and wished that no one else would either. He went back to his old idea that farming, as carried out in those days, was a wasteful way of producing food. More mechanization in the farming world would have to come. And—perhaps a little less than candid here—his sudden increase in the pay of his workers had been put into effect as "a plain act of social justice".

Ford's effort to increase the earnings of his thousands of workers might have been an act of justice; but it was an act of good sense too. As has already been seen, it gave him the pick of the skilled workers. What Henry was really trying to do was to calculate his likely profits in advance, and then give all the workmen an opportunity of sharing in those profits.

Another point, about which he said little, was that a high rate of wages would keep his workers loyal to the Ford Company. A big floating population of workers, with men changing their jobs very frequently, is not good for any employer. Any business founded on low pay, he knew, is likely to be a business which does not run smoothly. In 1914, before the plan for higher pay had been announced, Ford had been able to maintain his total of fourteen thousand workers at any one time only by recruiting over fifty thousand men within the whole of that year. This meant that men, on the whole, did not stay with the Ford Company for more than three or four months. In 1915, however, only about six thousand new men joined the company, and they were, for the most part, engaged because the amount of work being done, and the number of cars being sold, had increased steadily.

Nearly a million Ford cars had been sold by the middle of 1915. The Great War that had broken out in Europe did not, at first, have much effect on American business, for the United States, to begin with, kept aloof from the European conflict. The production of some eight hundred cars a day seemed such a wonderful effort that a far-off war in Europe did not so much as rise above the mental horizon of many Americans.

Henry Ford himself thought about it a lot, however. He had always believed that the most important thing in life was work; and work was an activity designed to help human beings. War, by contrast, was something that was designed to destroy human beings. As such, he detested it and felt that it was the worst thing that could possibly happen to the human race. It wastes life; it wastes food; it wastes all the other things, like ships and machines and motor-cars, which human ingenuity can make.

Henry Ford's opinion had already been canvassed by

117

the newspaper reporters on all the subjects which can be imagined. Naturally he commented on the war too. War, he held, was the result of human folly. Many people would have agreed with him on that. But he also regarded the outbreak of war in 1914 as, in the main, due to inefficient government on both sides of the European battle-front. No factory, he would say, could keep going, if those in charge of one department were forever quarrelling with those in charge of another. So his formula for ending the war was simple. Restore sensible management—which meant sensible government in the warring nations—and then the war would come to a halt.

His vast fortune—Ford was now making millions of dollars a year—enabled him to spend money advertising his ideas as well as his cars in the newspapers. Now he began taking a good deal of space to criticize all who were preparing for war, whether in the United States or outside it—and whether for a defensive war or an aggressive war. This upset many people, some of whom were his friends. There was a good deal of sympathy in the United States for Great Britain and France, and criticism of those who went to war in defence of their own rights or the rights of small nations was looked at very hostilely.

It is no real criticism of Henry Ford to say that, while an undoubted genius of an engineer, a designer and a businessman, he was far less inspired when he embarked on some political or international matter.

By 1915 he had produced a plan. The war, he said, was now hopelessly bogged down; neither side would be able to win; to have peace talks was the sensible way out. His advertisements stressed this, and there was a certain amount of good sense on his side. But there were many people who had liked Henry Ford in the past and who were now inclined to ask what these matters of high policy really had to do with a man whose task was making motor-cars.

Then Henry announced that he had chartered a ship, the *Oscar II*, and that he was proposing to sail for Europe, on a mission intended to bring peace to that troubled continent. "The time has come," he told a newspaperman, "to say 'Cease fire'."

He was in grim earnest about this. The ship, Henry announced, would be filled by peace-seekers, and the trip to Europe would be free of charge. The result of this offer was sure to be calamitous for the whole scheme, for a large number of people applied for places, and many of them were people with crazy or impractical ideas.

Henry's original scheme, for a negotiated peace, had some sense on its side. The peace-ship scheme was doomed to failure from the start. All kinds of squabbles broke out among the passengers. The ship enterprise was intended to end the trench warfare by Christmas, 1915. The aim was never within reach. Henry spent a few days ashore in Scandinavia; his passengers went on quarrelling violently. Then Henry left Europe on Christmas Eve, with the armies still deadlocked in France.

Henry Ford was now fifty-two years old. He was one of the richest men in the world. But people who saw him go off on that voyage in 1915, and who later saw him return, said that he was quite changed and now looked an old man, so sad was he that his efforts to snatch peace out of the jaws of war had failed.

It had not, however, caused him to lose popularity at home. There were those who thought he was talking dangerous nonsense when he attacked the men whom he saw as war-makers. But his name was put down in 1916 as a candidate for the American Presidency. The opening campaigns of an American presidential election are the State Primaries, when electors who have registered themselves as members of a particular political party vote to choose the candidate they want to represent that party. Anyone's name can be put down in these State Primaries, whether the candidate wishes to stand or not. Henry Ford did not wish to stand; but the State of Michigan put him at the top of the Poll. In the event he withdrew and said that he himself would be voting for Woodrow Wilson.

In 1917, the German Government announced submarine war on an unrestricted scale, and Henry realized that his previous efforts for peace had been utterly wasted. He went straight to Washington and offered the American Government the use of his Detroit plant to make whatever it thought would best help the fight against Germany.

The Government knew that it was in on a good thing. It ordered car parts, parts for artillery, and even steel helmets, which Ford made far more cheaply than anyone else. He announced that he did not propose to take a profit on any goods that he made for the Government in war-time. Some of his rivals in the engineering industry were not very happy about this. They knew that Ford's mass-production methods already enabled Henry to undercut most other firms; and if in addition he was to forgo all profit, he would make all the others look like profiteers.

According to one man who worked with him, and who wrote about him after his death, Henry Ford was once approached by an inventor with an idea for a new kind of engine, to be used in war-time. Henry said: "I can't do it. I have so many ideas of my own that I can't keep up with them. So how can I devote any time to yours?"

Certainly during those days of the First World War the Ford organization did much to help the government. One of Henry's ideas was to build small submarine-chasing ships. They were called "Eagle Boats" and were made to an American Navy design. Eagle Boats were wanted in large numbers as the campaign mounted by the Germans was stepped up after America came into the war. Henry Ford constructed a special long workshop at a new factory generally called the River Rouge plant, where the Eagle boats were built. They were about 200 feet (60 metres) long and 25 feet (7·5 metres) wide. The first was launched in July, 1918; two more were built in December, just after the Armistice ended the war. Henry was, after all, embarking on something quite fresh in building ships, and it was not his fault that large-scale production did not take place in time to have any direct effect on the war. Some sixty Eagle boats were eventually built; but the war was over by then, and they played no part in ending it. He had originally intended to build a boat a day; and if the war had not been won, there is little doubt that he would have achieved this aim. In one month in 1919 more than twenty were launched.

Before that, however, Henry was asked, in 1918, if he was prepared to stand as a candidate for the American Senate. He was, after all, one of the best-known men in the whole state of Michigan, and it appeared that he would stand a very good chance of being elected.

Henry Ford was the candidate put up by the Democratic Party, with the approval of President Wilson. The candidate for the rival party, the Republicans, was a man called Truman Newberry, who had in the past held office in the Government. The Republicans realized that in Henry Ford they had a worthy opponent, and they spent a very large amount of money on their campaign. This took place before the war had ended, and Henry's opponents, in their attacks on him, said that he was pro-German, and had employed many Germans in his works. All this had no real foundation in fact. But Henry was defeated.

Henry decided that all politics were a waste of time. He had tried to provide some sort of basis for peace, and it had failed; his peace ship had been laughed at. Now, when he had shown his willingness to serve his country in the Senate, it appeared that his country did not want him. He gave up all hope of doing anything in politics.

His task was to keep his business going as efficiently as possible, and this he was only too delighted to do.

The Eagle boats had not helped to win the war, but in making them he had tried out a new kind of inspiration. All the pieces—keels, decks and other parts—had been pressed out of sheet steel in such a way that even the rivet-holes were punched ready for use. Ford was pleased with them.

Even more pleased was Ford when he started making tractors. From his early days on the farm he had been eager to show that machines could do much of the work still being done by men and horses. Now he had the opportunity of building some machines that would take over a good deal of the hard, slogging work.

These tractors, which Ford started building in 1917, were to be used in the United States. Large numbers of them, too, were exported to wartime Great Britain, where the Government had embarked on a vast programme of food production. German submarines had been sinking many of the ships bringing food to Britain, and the Government therefore decided to plough up much land which had been used for sporting or decorative purposes. Golf courses were put under the plough, and so were some of the large parklands which were attached to the bigger country houses.

Most British farmers were still using horses for plough-ing; and the number of horses available was, of course, limited. The Government felt that machines could take over a good deal of the work that horses had been doing, and got into touch with Henry Ford as soon as news filtered through about the efficiency of the tractors which he was building in Detroit.

Ford at first offered to lend the British the full working drawings his factories were using. He said he would allow Ford tractors to be made in Britain free of charge, without demanding a royalty on each one made (the normal practice in the engineering industry). Some of the American-built tractors were tried out on British farms with great success, and for a time there was a suggestion that Ford tractors might be manufactured at the recently built Manchester factory, which was turning out large numbers of Ford cars, most of them assembled from parts made on the other side of the Atlantic. But some of the raw materials needed in making the tractors were in short supply in Britain, and the Manchester factory would have required a lot of alteration before it could be switched over from assembling cars to building tractors, so, after all, Henry decided to make them in Detroit. He was therefore given a British Government contract for five thousand of his tractors. These were shipped to Britain, and were already in use on British farms before many had been delivered to the farmers of America. At the end of the war the British Government expressed its deep gratitude to Henry for his help in keeping British food production going.

The tractor Henry called the Fordson. It sold in huge quantities as soon as production could be stepped up to the required level, and it went a long way towards proving the wisdom of Henry's youthful dream. He had done away with the worst of the hard work which agriculture had always demanded from all who were engaged in it.

The tractor had many uses. It could, of course, pull a plough as efficiently as any team of horses had done. But Henry soon learned that it was used for all sorts of other jobs on farms, even to moving portable buildings from one place to another, and pulling up tree stumps.

So the war staggered to its end. When the Armistice with the Germans was signed on November 11, 1918, Henry felt that a very unhappy episode in the world's history had ended. But there were many new and difficult problems to be faced.

For one thing, many industrial plants had been geared

to making weapons and other things needed in the war. Now that the fighting had stopped, it was not always easy to switch production back to something that was needed for peace. Fortunately for Henry, he was not faced by the difficulties confronting some manufacturers, for his River Rouge plant was still well equipped for making both cars and tractors. The Model T Ford was still the most popular car in the world, and the Fordson tractor was building up its reputation. It had become a truly international farming tool.

One evening, just after the Armistice, Henry spoke quietly to Edsel.

"We'll have to pay more for our labour, son," he said.

"Why?"

"A lot of these agitators are about, saying that the working man has saved his country, and that now the wicked bosses—that's us!—are trying do to him out of his rightful dues. We've got to show those guys that they're wrong."

"Can we afford to pay more?" Edsel asked. The basic wage of five dollars a day had been continued all through the war.

"We've *got* to afford to pay more," Henry said.

"And what do you mean to do?" asked Edsel. Sometimes it seemed that his father maintained too tight a control on all that was going on in the Company. Henry Ford was a great man; but, like many great men, he sometimes felt that he knew all the answers to all the questions, and he would not allow those working with him to have any real say in the way in which things were run.

It was so this time. Edsel queried the financial basis of a quick step-up in the basic wage being paid to Ford workers. But his father laughed Edsel's fears to scorn.

"Six dollars a day from next month," Henry announced boldly. Once again he took this decision without referring to anyone, and even without going too closely into what effect such a wage bill would have on the prosperity of the Ford Motor Company.

Once more he was proved right in what he called his "hunch". Offering six dollars a day instead of five paid off. The Company made over seventy million dollars profit in 1919.

In the two or three years that followed there were difficulties in many businesses; but Henry did not worry. He was now employing nearly fifty thousand men. He was making nearly a million cars a year. In May 1921 the five-millionth Ford car was driven away from the factory. It was the greatest boom that the motor industry had ever known; and Ford was making more than half the cars sold in the whole of the United States, as well as exporting vast quantities to South America and to Europe.

Most of the component parts for the cars and the tractors were now made in the Ford factories. He even started making glass for windscreens and lamps, and making it cheaper than the glass specialists could do. A number of outside contractors did still make components for him; but he usually made some of the same articles himself, so that he could keep a careful check on the actual cost.

It was all flourishing. And it seemed likely that it would go on for ever. Henry Ford was not a financial genius; but he had, people said, the magic touch that turned everything he did into gold. Even when his chiefs of staff disagreed with him—and they often did—he smiled, disregarded what they said, and then went on his own way. His own way generally paid well and showed a profit.

Of course, he had many brilliant engineers working for him. But they had to obey his orders and do what they were told. It was Henry Ford, too, who personally recruited these men. By building up such a talented team he was able to keep the factory going at a time when many others in the automobile industry were feeling the pinch and even facing possible ruin.

For when the war ended, business became difficult. As Henry had said to Edsel, there were political trouble-makers about. Trade unions were getting stronger. Henry had never believed in trade unions. He was, he said, paying better wages than those which the trade unions were demanding. Why need the unions bother about him when he was already providing a higher standard of wages than any of his competitors?

Here, again, Henry Ford was the individualist. He went his own way, and knew that for him his own way was best.

He even started a new venture in a field he had never tried before. He bought a small railway—The Detroit, Toledo and Ironton Railroad. This had been running at a loss for years. But soon after Ford had taken it over, it showed a small profit. There were already other railway lines in the area—a regular network of them—but Henry used what had once been a decrepit little line to bring raw materials to his factories and to move the finished articles out.

People began to think of Henry Ford as a kind of in-dustrial miracle-worker. But now, in 1921, trouble lay ahead.

CHAPTER TEN

TROUBLE AHEAD . . . AND BEHIND

Henry Ford was not in any way a financial genius. He had prided himself on never living on borrowed money, never having to raise a bank loan, never asking the bank to allow him an overdraft. If he had made any such request, there is no doubt that any bank in the world would have been prepared to lend him money, for the Ford Motor Company was making large profits and appeared likely to continue to make profits for the foreseeable future.

Yet in the aftermath of the First World War many firms ran into trouble of one sort or another. Most of Henry's rivals in the motor trade found that they were facing difficulties. More than one went bankrupt. For a long time, indeed, Henry wondered if he would be able to keep his firm afloat. He had to borrow money from the bank eventually, mainly because some of those who bought cars did not pay at once, so that he had a lot of cash owing to him, and was really dependent on this cash in order to pay for his supplies of raw materials.

Some of this loan from the bank he was able to pay back at once. Some of it, in 1920 and 1921, he still owed. He also knew that, because of the vast profits that the Company was still making, he owed a lot to the Government in income tax. By now he had a number of factories and assembly plants in various parts of the country. They had all seemed worth-while when they were started, but many of them were now scarcely paying their way—and with Henry's policy of continuing to pay more than the usual wage to his workers, many men were now getting more than their labour was really worth.

In mid-1920 Henry cut the prices of his cars to the public. The ordinary Model T touring car now cost less than five hundred dollars. Other makers were putting up the prices of their cars; Henry, original as always, reduced his. But he found now that the public was holding back. People knew that most manufacturers were building up stocks. They knew, too, that Henry's reaction to falling stocks was usually to cut prices. So they hoped that even lower prices would come.

He also thought that the suppliers of steel and other raw materials were keeping the price too high. In wartime prices usually soar. Many industries were trying to hold these inflated wartime prices, whereas Henry Ford was intent on lowering the selling prices of his cars and tractors. When he went into the factory and saw the cars being assembled, he was conscious that he was accumulating so much stock that before long he would not have room for all the cars that were awaiting sale.

A decision had to be made. The position was getting quite desperate. Henry tried to see a way to ride the storm. He knew in his bones that if he could somehow contrive to get through the next few months he would once more be in a good position. But how to get through?

He talked to his senior staff. He talked to his son Edsel. He talked to his wife. They all sensed that Henry Ford was now anxious as he had never been before. He was sure in his heart that sooner or later the public would again start buying cars. And when they started the Ford would be the first car that they would turn to. But at present the public appeared to have stopped buying. The position was made worse by the very fact that the Ford cars which people already owned were so good. Instead of buying a new car, they made the old car last. The fact that the old car was one, or two, or five years old did not matter. It still ran, and its very excellence made the selling of new cars more difficult.

Then Henry made his decision. He made it with dramatic suddenness as he had made so many other decisions in the past. He would close the works down for a short time, to take stock and see just where he stood. In December, 1920, it was stated that the Ford Motor Company was to close its doors for a fortnight. In the end it remained closed for all of six weeks.

Those who had sneered at Ford in the past now sneered again. Ford was in real trouble, they said. He owed money right, left and centre. The factories up and down the country would never open again.

One banker, so the story went, called on Henry Ford and offered him a loan to tide him over the difficult period.

"We don't want to borrow money," Henry said patiently.

The banker explained that he knew the financial position of the Company, and was aware that some millions of dollars would be needed to get the Ford Motor Company through its difficulties.

"We don't want to borrow money," Henry repeated. Then he rang for his secretary, and asked her to show the banker to the door.

Henry then got in touch with all his agents. Most of them had some cars in stock. He told them that he wanted every effort made to clear the stocks. Only if all the money owing to him could be brought in quickly could he see his way through the wood, repay the money still owing and pay off his tax debts.

More than fifty thousand cars were sold in a month. In two or three months, with the works slowly coming into operation again, some millions of dollars had been raised in sales. Then he cut down his overhead costs drastically. He used the telephone less; he made his office staff smaller and more efficient. He did not give any of his workmen the sack; but he told them that they must be still more efficient. In a few months millions of dollars had piled up in the bank, and the Ford Motor Company was out of the wood.

Soon Ford was extending his financial empire. He bought a small coal-mine; he bought some timber forests; he built some ships to carry his cars across the Great Lakes to the Canadian ports. On his sixtieth birthday in 1923, only two years after the company had been almost on the rocks, seven thousand Ford cars were produced.

Henry Ford had many critics. Some of them said that he drove his workers too hard, that the conveyor-belt was made the master of the men. That there was a certain amount of truth in this, it is not easy to deny. But the fact remains that he was continuing to pay his workers more than almost any other employer in the country, and that he had done this even in the difficult days of 1920 and 1921.

In 1923 there was even a move to get him made President of the United States. By the summer of that year so strong was the feeling that one Senator—a very shrewd man on political issues—said that if the election had taken place there and then, Ford would have swept the country. He was well in the lead with the voters, even though he himself had stated that he had no desire whatever to stand.

"Can you see us in the White House, Clara?" he asked his wife.

She shook her head sadly. "That I can't, Henry," she said.

It would, in fact, have made little difference if she had decided the other way. Henry had made up his mind not to run, and when Henry Ford made up his mind, it stayed made.

At Dearborn he built laboratories and experimental workshops where new-style engines might be tried out and tested. In the laboratory building he had a large room turned into a ballroom, and dances were often held there. He started farming again. He had his farm as highly mechanized as it could be. And he made the farm pay its way.

He decided that some of the American past was being lost. So rapid was progress that many famous old buildings —landmarks of history—were being destroyed. Henry, in the intervals of all his other tasks, decided that he would do his best to save some of these old places from destruction.

So he bought an old inn in Massachusetts, which had been the scene of Longfellow's *Tales of a Wayside Inn*. Also associated with Longfellow, the popular American poet, was a blacksmith's shop, supposed to have been the place where the spreading chestnut tree described in one of his most famous verses had grown. This too Henry bought, and had restored to something like its original state. He laid out more money in buying a little country schoolhouse, alleged to be that to which Mary's little lamb had followed her, according to the nursery rhyme.

Some of these things caused Henry's friends to grin broadly. The old man was reaching his second childhood, they said. It was not really so. He had more money now, and he was also conscious of the fact that the factory, with his skilled engineers and office staff, was more or less running itself; it only needed his attention when decisions were sought on some important point of policy. So he was free to enjoy more leisure.

Long ago he had told a newspaper interviewer that his hobby was work. In his early days this was no doubt true enough. But now he had many hobbies, and the means to follow them up.

Soon he started on another hobby. This was the buying of antiques—not only furniture, but vehicles and other relics of the early days of American history. He had all

131

these things sent to Dearborn, where he got no end of fun out of seeing to their arrangement.

Henry was aiming at collecting a really comprehensive display of souvenirs of early American history. His museum at Dearborn was to give visitors a new and exciting picture of American life as it had been lived a century and more previously.

All this division of his energy made him blind to one point, in the days from 1923 onwards. The Model T had been the greatest success that the motor world had ever seen. Now it was beginning to lose some of its popularity. Henry would not see it.

Edsel saw it. But he could not persuade his father to face the facts, though the two of them—father and son—were now sole owners of a company estimated as being worth more than a hundred million dollars.

"Don't you think we need a new model, Pop?" Edsel would ask sometimes.

"A new model. Why?" growled his father.

"Well, the old Ford looks a bit old-fashioned when you put it alongside a new Chevrolet or Plymouth," Edsel would retort.

"What does it matter if it does *look* old-fashioned?" asked Henry. "It's as reliable as ever. Haven't we improved the design a bit from time to time? Doesn't it give you far better speed with safety than it did five or ten years ago?"

"Maybe it does," agreed Edsel. "But what about the colour?"

"Colour?" Henry was quite puzzled at this criticism.

"Yes. You see other cars that are blue or grey or red or green—almost any colour you like to choose."

"You can paint a car in stripes of all the colours of the rainbow," said Henry. "That won't make it run any better."

"I guess not. But it may make it sell a lot better," answered Edsel.

Henry was, however, as obstinate as ever. The Ford fortune had been built on the Model T car, and he was quite sure that this car would continue to sell as well as it had ever done.

Edsel had ideas, too, about producing aircraft. He was sure that this would be the mode of travel in the future; if he could only start making aeroplanes, this would be an outlet for his energy and a new means of making money for the Company. Old Henry was against it, though he was to change his mind on this point in the years ahead. For the moment Ford cars and Fordson tractors were enough, in his opinion, to keep the Company as busy as it could well be. To begin building aeroplanes would be extending things a little too far, since it would mean even bigger workshops and assembly sheds.

There were now nearly ninety Ford plants, of one sort or another, in many different parts of the world. Thirty of them were outside the United States. If all these ran at their full capacity, they would be capable of turning out some two million cars every year.

The mass-production system was now in general use in many different industries, but Ford was regarded as its pioneer. He still speeded up the conveyor-belt whenever he could, and this still brought down criticism on his head—sometimes a disgruntled worker would even say that the belt had been so speeded up that no man could possibly work it.

Soon, however, Henry came to agree with Edsel that there might be something in his idea of building aircraft. An airfield was built at Dearborn, and the Ford Trimotor was put into production. This was a small three-engined aeroplane designed to carry freight rather than passengers. It was soon in the service of the American Post Office, carrying mail long distances, and sometimes penetrating to places which ordinary delivery methods could only reach at considerable intervals. The Ford Trimotor could deliver deep in the forests, providing an airstrip could be cleared, or far out on the wide-open prairie country. At the same time, Henry Ford was said to be keen on airships. The German Zeppelins had made a great impression in the First Great War, and Henry took them very seriously. He did not, however, try to build any after all—perhaps because he thought that they would be too clumsy for handling in any but the most enormous of factories.

Henry was now enjoying the experience of being a grandfather too. Henry Ford II, as he came to be called, the eldest son of Edsel Ford, was born on September 4, 1917. Edsel was resolved that young Henry should have a full education so, after his schooldays were over, the boy went to Yale, where he studied engineering and business management. It was almost predestined that he, too, would in the end enter the family business.

Old Henry was proud of his young grandson, though he was not yet sure exactly what the boy would achieve. Edsel was quietly certain that young Henry would be a great man in due course.

Meanwhile the Ford Motor Company went on. Henry was getting old, though his mind was as alert as ever. He grinned when he read in the papers that some new car was coming out in a vivid colour, or with a new body designed to cut down wind-resistance, or with a new system of gears or transmission. He dismissed all these things as fancy trimmings, which had little to do either with sales or with success on the roads.

Edsel's patience began to grow thinner. The Model T had been in production since 1911, and it was not, Edsel thought, natural that a car should continue virtually unchanged for twelve years and more. True, as his father had pointed out during that previous talk, there had been changes made—but they had been very minor ones, and they did not have any sort of effect on the appearance of the car. And the car-buying public was growing more conscious of the appearance of the vehicles it rode in than had ever been the case in the past.

There were rumours that the Ford model was going to be altered. These rumours started in 1925 or 1926. But they were always denied as soon as they began to spread.

One statement issued to the Press said that it was firm Company policy not to make any change which could not be worked into any car already existing. In other words, if a new model Ford did come out, any spare parts would be the same as the spare parts already in use with the Model T. This really froze production and prevented even the cleverest of engineers and designers in the Ford factory from making anything but slight changes and improvements in the cars already being produced. Any new model was just out of the question.

The Ford agents, too, were now asking for a change. They were finding Ford cars more and more difficult to sell—and their living depended on their being able to sell cars in large numbers. Letters poured into Detroit pleading that a more modern-looking car should be produced. Only thus, the agents said, would they be able to maintain the level of sales which had been achieved, now, for years. The peak, it seemed, was from 1923 to 1925. During those years about two million Ford cars had been sold each year—a well-nigh incredible achievement. But in 1926 a sudden fall in demand took place.

"They're getting tired of us," Edsel said to his father. Edsel was now President of the Company, though control still remained largely in old Henry's hands.

"Getting tired of us? Rubbish!" snapped Henry.

"Well, look at the sales figures! They're going down month by month—almost week by week."

"Figures will pick up again, son," said Henry confidently. "We've had our ups and downs before. We've seen ourselves through sticky periods. We shall see ourselves through this one. You just wait."

135

The trouble was that Edsel could not wait. Each time sales figures came in they showed a further decline in the numbers of cars selling. The agents were getting worried as they found unsaleable cars piling up in their warehouses and showrooms.

"Just like 1920," Henry said, when this evidence was put in front of him. "We thought, then, that we should never see the end of the slump in sales—but we did."

"This is a worse slump than 1920," Edsel pointed out. "Then we were faced by the problem of the high price of materials after the war. Now prices are low—including the price of our cars—but we're not really getting anywhere at all. The cars are being made, they're being pushed out into the salerooms—and they're just sticking there. They aren't selling, Pop, you can't get away from that."

"They will sell again soon," Henry repeated grumpily. "Don't worry. It will be O.K. soon."

But it was not O.K. soon. Henry still held that there would be no change in the Model T. In February, 1927, he issued a statement to the papers saying that no drastic change in the cars being made by Fords was contemplated. The dealers greeted this statement with something not very far removed from alarm, since they already held large stocks, and knew that, as long as the Ford plants went on churning out cars, the stocks would increase and increase.

The number of Model T Fords now in existence was nearly fifteen million. It had been a wonderful achievement—the greatest achievement in the history of the car-making industry. But everyone except Henry Ford himself was now conscious that it was an achievement that must soon come to its end.

Arguments and discussion still went on—arguments and discussions with old Henry on one side, and his son and all the leading members of his staff on the other.

"It's no good, Mr. Ford," one of his senior staff would say. "We've got to face facts."

"I'm facing facts," Henry would say testily.

"I'm afraid that in this case you're not," the engineer pointed out. "The main fact is that the public will no longer buy Ford cars of the old design."

"Why not? It's a good design."

"It *was* a good design," the engineer stated. "Ten or fifteen years ago it was a very good design indeed. It is still a good reliable car with a fine engine. But, Mr. Ford, it looks old-fashioned."

"Huh! Looks! What do the looks of the car matter, as long as it is simple to drive, and it runs well?" Henry asked.

"I'm afraid that looks mean an awful lot to the present-day car buyer," said the engineer. "This is not the year 1911, Mr. Ford. This is the year 1927, and conditions have changed."

There were endless conferences and discussions of this kind. Henry was stubborn and difficult to move. He still held a majority holding of the shares, which meant that there could be no change in policy without his consent. To get him to agree to altering the basic policy of the Company was the toughest job that Edsel and the heads of the various departments had ever faced in their lives.

Several times they felt that they had Henry on the verge of agreeing. Then he would draw back and suddenly refuse. "No!" he would say. "If they don't like our cars, they can leave them alone."

"That's just what they're doing," Edsel pointed out. "They're leaving them alone."

Finally, however, they managed to get him to agree. Overborne and weary from much argument, Henry agreed that the Model T should no longer continue in production.

Henry's final consent came three months after he had stated that no drastic change in policy was being contemplated. This was as drastic a change as could be imagined.

But the Model T was undoubtedly Henry Ford's greatest achievement. Fifteen million cars of this design were built. The fifteen-millionth Henry decided to keep as a souvenir.

Henry Ford and Edsel drove that car from Detroit to Dearborn, on a day of pouring rain. Just as a gesture they had the hood down, and they got soaking wet. But this was their way of marking the end of an era in motoring history.

CHAPTER ELEVEN

CHANGES AND CHANCES

The death of the Model T was in part the death of Henry Ford. He had made this famous old car his pet; and even though he still attended meetings and discussions in Detroit and Dearborn, his heart was not in them as it had been in days gone by.

The immense reorganization that followed the abandonment of the Model T was something that occupied all the senior staff for a long time. Henry himself, now aged sixty-four, did not take as much interest in the matter as he would have done a few years earlier. There were now Ford factories in many countries. They had all been designed to make or to assemble one type of car. Now they had all to be re-geared to a different model.

Gradually, however, Henry recovered his interest. A new car had to be designed. One or two of the new-style models must then be made by hand. These prototypes had to be tried out. The proof of the pudding was in the eating, and the proof of the car was on the road. New equipment had to be sent all over the world as soon as the new model was approved. The assembly-lines had to be re-designed; tools, to stamp out new parts from sheet metal, had to be made by the thousand. It was an operation so huge that most men would have quailed. But once Henry had come to terms with the loss of the Model T, he started studying all the new things that would have to be done. He knew that the change-over would be an immensely expensive affair. (When at last it had all been put into effect, it was calculated that its cost had been not much short of a hundred million dollars, all told.)

The River Rouge factory was the place where the new model was to be made. The old Highland Park factory could carry on making spare parts for the Model T. Henry knew—who knew better?—that the millions of cars which had come from the Ford factories would need spare parts and servicing for many years. The new car would ultimately replace the Model T; but Henry knew how dependable the older car had been, and was very much aware that he would have to provide spare parts for a good many years ahead.

At River Rouge the changes were enormous. Thirty miles of new conveyor-belts had to be fitted up. And new problems arose. All Henry's rivals and competitors, naturally, wanted to know what the new car would be like. Henry feared spies from rival firms. Pressmen from daily papers and from the engineering journals swarmed around the plant. To keep all these people at bay was not easy. Meanwhile the decisions had to be taken. What would the new model be like? What horse-power? What style of body? What colour would it be painted? There was a host of problems to be dealt with. Henry was now visibly ageing; but he was still the major force in the firm, and still kept his finger on almost every detail.

There were many rumours about the new car. Various experimental models were tried out on the roads, some of them driven by Henry himself. News of what the car was like was leaked out to the Press.

Before anyone had even seen the new car no fewer than four hundred thousand of them were on order. The new model was called Model A and was a much more modern-style car than the old Model T had been.

On December 1, 1927, Fords spent over a million dollars in advertising the new car all over the United States, in two thousand different newspapers. On December

2, sample cars were to be on show. The main Ford show-room in New York was so besieged by members of the public that the police had to call out extra reserves to keep the queues moving slowly past, staring at the new cars on display within. Once again Henry Ford had succeeded in hitting the headlines. He had spent a million dollars in advertising; but the free publicity which the Press gave him was worth many times that amount.

A year from that first public appearance of the Model A the factories were turning out something like six thousand cars a day. The number of workers reached out towards two hundred thousand. Once again a Ford gamble had paid off. Henry was compelled to admit that, though he had fought against this change all the way, it had been completely justified. Fords had looked like a spent force, but now they were back in the very forefront of the motor-ing world. Before long the hundred million dollars that had been spent on re-organization would be replaced.

But there were new troubles ahead for American indus-try as a whole. There had been booms and slumps before. But the biggest slump ever known was to hit the business world in 1930. To begin with, Henry Ford, now not far from seventy years of age, was not unduly disturbed. He had seen business problems before, and had overcome them. The fact that this slump appeared to be more widespread than any previous ones did not necessarily mean that the Ford Motor Company was going to suffer as a result.

Henry was now getting some of his scientific staff working on the possibility of making synthetic rubber. He thought that this might result in a considerable saving in the making of tyres. At the same time he invested some money in rubber plantations in Brazil, thus ensuring that if the synthetic rubber did not, after all, prove successful, he would have a supply of natural rubber readily available.

In 1929 he had sent his son Edsel over to England, to

cut the first sod on a piece of wet marshland at Dagenham in Essex. This was the beginning of what was to be the largest Ford factory overseas. An English company was set up to undertake the running of this English factory; but the majority of the shares were still held in Dearborn, so the policy of the English factory was settled by Henry and his American associates. A similar scheme was followed in other countries, ranging from Holland to Japan and from Germany to Mexico.

This overseas development, which Henry followed with increasing interest, was to some extent slowed up by the great business slump of 1930. The effect on Fords was not as great as on some firms. In 1931 the twenty millionth Ford car was made. Sales of the Model A held up better than most in the difficult financial conditions of the time. And Henry, now that he had been persuaded to change his old policy of not allowing any radical alterations to a model in production, improved the Model A year by year.

To begin with, there were few drastic changes, although Henry did agree to the car's being made a little larger. This made it a little heavier than before, which rather went against Henry's belief in a light-weight car; but the engine was so efficient that the extra weight did not cause any reduction in speed. Henry justified his changes of opinion by saying that when a man gets too old to change, he dies. Henry was resolved that he was not going to die yet.

Then there came the biggest change of all. The cars which Henry had marketed up to now had all—since the earliest days—been four-cylinder cars. Now Henry decided that an eight-cylinder car, to be called the V8, should be made. "After all," he said, "an eight-cylinder engine is only like two four-cylinder ones, isn't it?"

Gone, now, was the old Ford image altogether. The V8 was to be available in no fewer than fourteen different colours. There was one thing about old Henry, people

142

said; when he changed his mind over something, he certainly changed it good and properly. The new car could do over eighty miles an hour, and even at such a speed the driver and his passengers were comfortable. Gone, too, was the old jeer about Ford cars being rattletraps. The Model T had been liable to rattle; but the V8, if not as silent as a Rolls-Royce, was as quiet as most people could have desired.

The slump still went on. Even some of the Ford factories had to close down. Henry remained optimistic. He was sure that his country would get through this difficult time, as it had got through other difficult times earlier in its history.

He made himself unpopular, however, by refusing to co-operate in the National Recovery Act—the so-called "New Deal"—which was being put into operation by Franklin Roosevelt, the President. This act gave the President the right, for the time being, to take control of finance, industry, and business. Henry objected. He was not going to let the Government tell him how to run his business, which he had now done with great efficiency for a good many years.

The National Recovery Act did something, too, to regulate wages. Henry felt he did not need anyone to regulate the wages he was paying—he had always paid more than the market rate. This was true. And the sturdy and independent old man felt that he was perfectly justified in refusing to have any direct connexion with the "New Deal". He obeyed all the laws, but his refusal to endorse the President's policy made him long unpopular in Government circles. And this, combined with the fact that his assembly-line methods made it seem his workers operated under high pressure, made some political thinkers very critical of what he was doing.

Eventually, as Henry had felt certain would happen, the United States recovered from the depth of the business

143

depression, though it was 1934 before the business world returned to something like normality. In January, 1934, Ford sold over fifty-seven thousand cars—the biggest sales figures that had been reached for more than two years. Some of the assembly plants which had closed down in 1932 were now re-opened.

Henry, in an effort to get publicity, again started entering some of his cars in races and other sporting events. At a stock-car meeting in Los Angeles in 1934 twenty-two of the twenty-six cars taking part were Fords—a tribute to their road-worthiness, and their stability.

All too soon, however, the war clouds began to gather over Europe again. Hitler, the German Chancellor, seemed to be threatening the peace of the world. Henry Ford, however, was once more the optimist. "War is on its last legs," he said, explaining that present-day methods of warfare would kill the civilians behind the lines, as well as the soldiers and sailors and airmen. "That will stop it," he added.

Long, long ago Henry was reported to have said that history was bunk. It is still the most widely quoted of all his many sayings, and it appears that he believed it. More sensible was one historian's remark to the effect that all we learn from history is the fact that men do not learn from history. This certainly applied to Henry Ford. Although he had lived through the First World War, and had seen the utter failure of his own attempt to bring good sense and peace to the warring nations, he still did not realize, as 1939 drew nearer, that Europe was again treading the path she had trodden in 1914. He even said, when war broke out on September 3, 1939, that it would not last long, because the United States would not get involved. When the First World War had begun, twenty-five years earlier, he had also thought that the United States could avoid the conflict. He had not understood then, and he did not understand now, that it was all but impossible for the

United States to avoid entanglement in any big European war.

Henry Ford's genius did not extend to understanding international affairs. To begin with, in 1939, he refused to make aeroplane engines in the United States for the British Government, though a plan had been discussed by which Fords in Detroit would make Rolls-Royce engines for the fighter aircraft which were defending the shores of Britain. Edsel Ford had, indeed, agreed to the scheme, but Henry, at the age of seventy-six, still had the right to take the final decisions in such matters. He refused. There could be no appeal against his decision. It seems there was a curious blind spot in Henry's brain which affected his reactions at the beginning of each of the two Great Wars. He changed only when America became directly involved in the conflict.

Henry's experience in building aero-engines was not wide. He always said that in this, as in all other fields of engineering, the important matter was to get an agreed design, and then stick to it. Only thus would it be possible to use mass-production methods. Given a firm design for an engine, Henry said, he could turn out a thousand a day; though this was rather a wild and exaggerated estimate. But the men who were fighting the war knew that they would have to try prototype engines out in actual combat before finalizing the design—and even then there might be alterations to meet new combat conditions or to counteract changes in the design of the enemy machines with which they were in conflict.

As soon as the Japanese raid on Pearl Harbour had taken place, and the United States had been brought into the war, Henry's philosophy changed as suddenly as it had done in 1917. He was at once given a number of government contracts, the first being one for building aero-engines for the United States Government's use. The order was welcome; but there appeared to be no suitable factory available. Henry knew that the engines were wanted quickly; a firm design had already been approved. There was, as far as he could see, only one thing to do. The River Rouge factory had a huge carpark, for almost all the workers now drove to work every day. The car park was smooth and concreted. Here was a place, after all, where a sizeable factory could be run up quickly.

"Clear the cars off," Henry ordered. "Let them park wherever they can."

There were many grumbles from the workers, but Henry did not let that worry him at all. On what had been a car park a huge new factory soon arose. Here thirty-three acres (thirteen hectares) were covered in; and here aero-engines soon came into production.

Thirty miles from Detroit was a district called Willow Run. Here Henry proposed to build another factory where parts for bombers could be made and assembled. There was much criticism of this factory—it was once nicknamed "Never run", because it seemed such a long time before it came into full-scale production. Henry's critics conveniently forgot that the place had been an ordinary stretch of farming land; it took time to adapt it and to build a factory of the most modern type.

In all these projects Edsel Ford had been at his father's side. Now, at long last, it seemed that Henry was giving his son his head, allowing him to take some of his own decisions. In 1938, Edsel's son, Henry Ford II, had also joined the Board of Directors of the Ford Motor Company, though he had been serving in the American Navy from 1941 onwards.

Henry had in most respects been fortunate in his family relationships; but in 1943 there came a sad and tragic loss. Edsel Ford had suffered at intervals from gastric ulcers, which had given him much pain and had caused him to observe the strictest possible diet. Now he fell seriously ill, and even though an earlier operation for ulcers had been successful, the doctors now found something far worse. It was a stomach cancer from which Edsel Ford died in May, 1943. He was only forty-nine years old. Henry was now nearly eighty.

Whatever his age, Henry never shirked responsibility. He was heartbroken over the loss of his son—as, of course, was Mrs. Ford. But he knew that his Company was of the greatest possible importance to his country. He knew, too, that unless it was kept working smoothly there might be a collapse, which would hurt the country as much as it hurt Fords.

Putting his grief behind him, then, he went back to his office and buried himself in the work that was waiting for him. Some of the senior members of the firm had left his employ, since they had found it difficult to fit in with wartime conditions. They might also have found it difficult to fit in with an elderly chief who still wanted to have his own way! This meant that Henry did not have as many able assistants as he had had earlier. Yet he knew that he would have to keep things going. His grandson was now twenty-six years of age, but he was serving in the Navy and even could he be brought back from his naval service, his practical experience of the Company was not yet great.

The whole organization of the vast Ford empire therefore now fell on the shoulders of an old man, getting increasingly frail as the years rolled by. Yet still he kept up the routine of his life. He got up at half-past five in the morning. He wandered around his garden before breakfast. He set off for work at eight o'clock and spent a long and laborious day in conferences with his staff, and in seeing what was going on at Willow Run or at River Rouge. It was a hard life for an old man, but he would not have changed it in any detail. The life of the Ford Motor Company was the life of Henry Ford. In one interview which he gave to a newspaper man when he was over eighty years of age, he said: "Go to work. That's the

147

answer to everything." For Henry Ford, it *was* the answer to everything. Idleness was the source of all evil for him. And if this meant that many worth-while human activities passed him by, he managed none the less to accomplish what he set out to do. He probably had little taste for literature or art or music. But the "frills on life", as he might have said, were never able to hold a man of his special kind of genius.

On his eightieth birthday Ford said that he did not think of the day as ending his eightieth year, but as beginning his eighty-first. But he was getting old, none the less. Though not much mention was made of it at the time in the public Press, Henry Ford had suffered a stroke in 1938. He had apparently made a complete recovery, but there was always a chance that another such illness might follow. And, since he was still more or less a dictator at the Ford Motor Company, a second stroke, in those crucial days of war effort, might have landed the Company, and even the American nation, in severe difficulties. Some of his senior staff therefore quietly communicated this fear to the Government, and asked if it would be possible to release Ford's grandson from the Navy, where he had been serving with some distinction, so that he would be at hand to take over control of the Ford empire should the need arise.

This was readily agreed, and so Henry Ford II returned to Detroit and was appointed Vice-President of the Company, still under the direction of his grandfather.

Henry Ford II was a young man of power of character, who was in due course to make a considerable mark on the policy of the Company, though in his first days as Vice-President he had to a large extent to follow his grandfather's lead. Old Henry had, after all, nursed the Company from its earliest days, and seen it build up into the huge concern which it now was. He had also undertaken a good deal of the negotiating in the drawing up of the various government contracts which formed, for the time being, the main part of the responsibilities of the Ford Motor Company. But Henry's grandson soon learned all that there was to be known about the work of the Company. By going around the plant with his grandfather day by day, he taught himself, being a very observant person, exactly what was going on. Perhaps he sometimes found his grandfather rather frustrating, as no doubt Edsel had done over the years, but he still admired him and found him a man whose example was to be followed in many important respects.

Old Henry, too, was proud of his grandson. Perhaps he sometimes disagreed with points which the young man might make in the course of a discussion or a business conference, but he was compelled to admit that his grandson was a highly intelligent young man, and a man of clear-cut and sensible views.

Ford's early days, when he was dreaming of the development which was destined to produce a new sort of road transport, were days of hard, slogging work and comparative poverty. Then, once he had established himself as the most successful automobile manufacturer in the world, he became a world-leader and a world-beater in his field. In those years—which ran roughly from 1913 to 1925—he was a great figure admired by almost all who had any dealings with him. Some people criticized him; some people thought him wrong-headed and even wrong-hearted. But he was still a man of real genius, and perhaps the most noteworthy example in modern history of a pioneer who changed the whole social habits of a nation.

It was in the days following his triumph that Henry Ford proved to differ from the majority of men of genius. There can be few men in the whole history of the world who manage to maintain virtual control of a great business into their eighty-first year. And in that eighty-first year, Henry Ford was almost a national institution in the

United States. His press interviews became more and more famous. His pawky sense of humour brought many a chuckle to the breakfast tables of America, for his sayings were widely reported in the newspapers. And he enabled the American nation to contribute to the defeat of Nazism in a far more effective fashion than might have been possible had he not lived.

That he would not have much longer in control of his Company when once the war had been won became more and more obvious to his grandson and to those who knew something of the internal workings of the firm. Old Henry himself, it would appear, did not think about this at all. He was content to live day by day, doing all the tasks that came his way, to go home at night and chat to his wife, as he had chatted to her nearly every evening now for sixty years. Clara still admired him as she had done from the beginning. By now she understood him as no one else had ever done. Perhaps she sometimes thought that he was making a mistake, but she did not bother to say so. She knew in her heart that his mistakes were few and far between, and that what he had done could have been done by no one else in the world.

CHAPTER TWELVE

LAST DAYS

Old Henry had his doubts about the aftermath of the Second World War. He remembered the slump that had hit the world in 1921, and he sometimes wondered if a similar industrial tragedy might come when the war against the Nazis had been brought to a successful conclusion. Many Americans felt doubtful about the actual outcome of the war: Henry never had any doubts on that score, but he was often concerned about subsequent developments. He warned his grandson that unless they made careful preparation for the switchover to peacetime production, the Ford Motor Company might be in for grave trouble when hostilities ended.

Henry Ford II was too intelligent a man not to have thought of this himself. The younger man, while he knew of the wonderful success of the older models, had little doubt that when peace again arrived, newer models would be needed—and quickly.

Old Henry was getting weary as the war drew near to its end. He was now concentrating on all sorts of hobbies and side-interests. The museum, which he had dedicated to the memory of Edison, the inventor who had been of great encouragement to him in days gone by, proved one of his supreme interests. Among his new ideas was one prompted by the fact that he had helped in the building of several churches; he came out with the suggestion that churches should not just be reserved for use at the Sunday services, but should serve as social and educational

151

centres during the week. All religions, he said, should be encouraged to get together somehow for a common purpose. Always a religious man, Henry Ford was not a bigoted man. He wished for greater tolerance and co-operation between the followers of different faiths; and at Dearborn, too, he tried to work out a way in which he could help to build up a real centre for social fellowship.

In 1945 the war ended. Old Henry, content that America and her allies had emerged victorious, came to see that the time was fast approaching when he would have to give up his active life within the Ford Motor Company. It was in some respects a sad moment for him, as it must be for most men when they retire. But in his letter of resignation he said that he would be glad to remain on the Board of Directors and to serve as an expert adviser.

The other directors did not wish Henry to leave the service of the Company. His knowledge of the whole background of automobile manufacture was such that he would undoubtedly be of the greatest value to the Company for the rest of his life. But at the same time they no doubt felt some relief that the old man would no longer settle every detail of policy and over-ride younger men whose experience of the public's taste was more up-to-date than his. It was in September, 1945, that Henry Ford, owner of the greatest name in automobile history, stepped down from the Presidency of the Company he had created years before. More than sixty years had gone by since he had started his work on engines. From his original idea had grown a company which was one of the most prosperous in the world. Founded in 1903, it had been based on old Henry's ideas and "know-how". Now he was to give up his exalted position as the President of the firm, and to resume his old place as one of the rank-and-file directors.

There was little doubt who would follow Henry as President of the Company. The Ford Motor Company had always been a closely-knit family business, with the bulk of the shares being held by various members of the Ford family. Now, as old Henry stepped down, it was clear that young Henry would step up.

Henry Ford II was one of the most promising young men in the industrial world of the mid-twentieth century. As his grandfather gave up the reins, young Henry Ford was twenty-eight years old. His grandfather was only too pleased to hand over the main control of the business to a young man so promising and so talented. All the same, old Henry made it very clear that he was not resigning the Presidency of the Company because he was worn out, physically or mentally. He explained in a public statement that he was now concerned to devote most of his time to various personal interests.

Needless to say, he watched the progress of the Company. More especially, he watched the progress of his grandson in the presidential chair.

But the museum, the farm, the folk-dancing classes—these were Henry's new interests. The museum very soon took up a large proportion of his time . . . and his income. There was, for example, a full-scale reproduction of The Rocket, the famous old locomotive designed and built by George Stephenson. As a pioneer of road transport, Henry Ford had a healthy respect for the pioneers of rail transport. There were, of course, many cars in that museum too: a number of early Fords, and early models made by other firms, including the Mercedes which had been the property of the German Emperor during the First Great War.

Then Henry devoted his attention to Greenfield Village —a group of exact replicas of historic American buildings. Henry's birthplace was taken to pieces, carried off to Greenfield, and there put together again; so was the schoolhouse in which the future motor king had received his early education. It was not purely an American village, however. Henry bought two cottages in the English Cotswolds, had them taken down, stone by stone, and then rebuilt in Greenfield. He had begun building the village before the outbreak of the Second Great War. But, as he gave up the Presidency of his firm, Henry was able to devote more time, attention and money to it.

As far as the Company was concerned, he was involved with its day-to-day workings a lot less after his grandson became President, though he still took a deep interest in its welfare. He was glad to hear that the great Ford plant at Dagenham in Essex was flourishing, producing cars by the hundred thousand. The fact that the models being made, in the United States, in Great Britain, and in other countries, were now very different from the old Model T no longer worried Henry. He had come to see that times changed, and that men had to change with the changing times. In the years ahead there came into being the Ford Popular, the Ford Anglia, the Ford Cortina, the Ford Escort and many another Ford car—all very different from those which had been marketed in the early days of the Company, but all owing a good deal, indirectly at least, to the genius of Henry Ford.

All his life Henry Ford regarded his success as something which brought with it responsibilities as well as advantages. He made vast sums of money, but he thought of himself as holding that money in trust. At any time he could have launched his Ford Motor Company as a public concern, asking the public to subscribe for shares, and could have sold out, in effect, for many millions of dollars. That he kept Fords a family business was not so much due to a desire to keep a huge fortune within family control as to a wish to use his fortune to help some of the less fortunate human-beings. In 1936 he had started a charitable body called the Ford Foundation. During Henry's lifetime it tended to use its vast resources for rather narrow aims; but Henry had also looked to the future, and after his death the Ford Foundation helped all sorts of worth-while causes, including literary work and scientific research.

His last years were, it would seem, fairly happy ones. He still took an interest in his farm. He still bought many important historical relics for his museum. He still attended board meetings, seeing his grandson taking the chair, and putting forward, from time to time, ideas of his own which revealed that his genius was by no means exhausted.

One thing that Henry Ford II did which his grandfather did not altogether approve, was to come to better relations with the trade unions, which old Henry Ford had so strenuously opposed for so many years. Old Henry was an individualist. He disapproved of too much tight organisation, whether of labour forces or of boards of directors. He felt, all through his business life, that any arrangements that might be made, between the employers and the employed, should be purely personal arrangements, varying from firm to firm and from one situation to another. This often brought him into conflict with the unions. Sometimes it even brought him into conflict with the Government. But the fact that this often put him in a difficult position did not alter his respect for a good worker. Nor, for that matter, did it alter the respect which the general public had for him.

People generally admire a man who is thought to be a "character". Henry Ford was often looked on as a kind of genial eccentric, whose amusing traits of character led him to say and do many foolish things. But he was still regarded with respect by millions of people, in the United States and in many countries overseas.

When he finally resigned his position as President of the Company which he had done so much to build up, he was over eighty years of age. There can be few men who have lived an active life to such advanced years.

Everyone who knew him thought that he would go on being active for a long time to come. "Henry Ford will

155

live to be a hundred," people said. He seemed to be a permanent part of the American scene, one of those men who have always been there, and seem likely to continue to be there for ever.

Yet, all the time, he was growing more frail. After his stroke in 1938 he continued to get weaker in body, though his brain remained as active as ever. It was no doubt the death of Edsel that dealt him the cruellest blow, though the need to serve the United States in the Second Great War kept him going, even when he was conscious that his strength was declining.

After his grandson took over in 1945 Henry grew visibly weaker. There was still the twinkle in the eye. There was still the sudden flash of insight when some new business proposition came up for discussion. But, in spite of the great care taken of him by Clara, his wife, he seemed to sink as the years went by.

By 1947 it was clear to all who knew him that he had not long to live. Yet he still showed signs of energy. In April that year there was torrential rain around Dearborn. The Rouge River overflowed its banks, and floods drew near to Henry's house. Henry went out and inspected the flood damage, paying especial attention to the places where it appeared to be drawing dangerously near the great factory. To some of those who spoke to him on April 7, 1947, he seemed to be much his own self.

Clara was not so sure. She thought that he was weakening. But she did not dare to criticize him, or point out that he was taxing his waning strength too much in walking about studying the flooded land and seeing if something could be done to keep the Ford plant in full-scale operation.

"I'll have another look around tomorrow," he announced to his wife when he got home. "I guess we'll pull through if the floods don't get any worse—and I think the water is going down a bit."

156

But the water had cut off electric power from the house. There was no electric light, and no electric fires. An old-fashioned paraffin lamp was alight in Henry's bedroom, and candles were dotted about the house. Log fires burned cheerfully in the fireplaces.

But Henry was tired. He went to bed at nine o'clock, and soon drifted off into a peaceful sleep. Perhaps he was amused that, owing to the floods, the house looked much like his childhood home, some eighty-three years before.

He woke at a quarter past eleven. "Could I have some water?" he asked. His wife, thinking that he looked far from well, brought him the drink. Then she sat by his bedside, looking anxiously at him. Within twenty-five minutes he was dead. A brain haemorrhage had killed Henry Ford.

An era in American industry was over. The greatest man in the motor trade was no more. But as long as anyone remembers the Model T Ford, Henry will not be forgotten. Perhaps he felt that his greatest achievement ended when the Model T went out of production. But, even though he lived for years after that date, the fact remains that transport throughout the world would have been very different had Henry Ford not lived.